Gouldian finch

Gouldian Finches as Pets

Gouldian Finches Keeping, Pros and Cons, Care, Housing, Diet and Health.
by

Roger Rodendale

Table of Contents

Introduction

Also known as the Lady Gouldian, the Gouldian Finch is one of the most colorful birds of the family. Naturally these birds are found in a variety of colors that are strikingly beautiful. These small birds are preferred pets because of their size and their beauty.

These birds are not exactly fond of human handling. They prefer to spend most of their time within their cages. However, they have extremely soothing voices that have made them a popular choice as pets.

Gouldian Finches are perfect pets for homes with children and the elderly because of their peaceful and quiet nature. They are great apartment birds thanks to their size. However, for anyone who wants a bird that they can pet and play with, this may not be the ideal choice.

Learning to care about these birds is extremely important before you bring them home. They are quite unlike other pet birds because they do not really form strong bonds with their owners as most other pet birds do.

These birds also have specific cage and food requirements that need to be met in order to keep them healthy. Gouldian Finches are particularly difficult birds to keep because there are very few instances of these birds being kept as a single bird. So, you will have to learn to take care of a small flock or at least a pair of these birds.

Showing Gouldian Finches is one of the most favorite activities of their owners. These beautiful birds can be entered into shows as well. They are tricky birds to train, however. Since they do not interact as much with humans, it is necessary for you to learn the right way to train these birds and work with them.

Whether you are interested in showing your Gouldian Finches or are just looking at a pet bird, this book can help you learn everything that you need to know about these birds. The book gives you all the details such as:

- Feeding the birds.
- Keeping them clean.
- Cage requirements and space requirements.
- Handling and caring for the birds.
- Basic hygiene of the cage.
- Understanding dynamics of the flock or pair.
- Breeding Finches.

There are several more subjects in this book that will guide you in the right direction when it comes to these birds. You will be able to keep your bird healthy and happy with the practical tips provided in this book.

Bringing a bird home is a big responsibility and you need to make sure that you take care of all their requirements. This book is the first step to doing that. You must make sure that you keep yourself updated with respect to the healthcare and other needs of the bird.

Having a pet bird at home is a great responsibility as you have to care for these birds for several years. You will also be required to manage and handle the quirks in personality that may come with each species. This book will also help you decide if the Gouldian Finch is, the right bird for you.

Chapter 1: Introduction to Gouldian Finches

Gouldian Finches are among the most fascinating birds. Although these birds are extremely shy, they are known to make wonderful pets. There are several myths surrounding this bird that usually makes people think twice before bringing them home. However, when cared for properly, these birds make for delightful pets.

Before you decide to bring a Gouldian Finch home, learning about the history and the natural habitat of the bird will do you a lot of good. This will help you understand specific needs of the bird and provide for the bird as needed.

1. Physical traits of Gouldian Finches

Gouldian Finches are extremely colorful birds, which has earned them the name, Rainbow Finch. These birds also go by the name of Lady Gouldian. The physical traits of the bird are as follows:

- **The size:** Gouldian Finches are small birds with an average size of about 4.7 to 5.9 inches. This size includes the length from the head to the tip of the tail. Typically, a Gouldian Finch will weigh about 14 to 15 grams when fully grown.

- **Plumage:** The first thing that you will notice about the Gouldian Finch is the brightly colored plumage. These birds occur in a variety of colors naturally. The color of the feathers range from black, yellow, green, red to several others.

The coloration of the head is used to distinguish between the different types of Gouldian Finches. It was initially believed that only three types of Gouldian Finches exist in the wild. However, several colorations have been discovered in the wild.

In addition to that, selective breeding has also lead to mutations in the coloration of the body and the color of the chest.

- **Beak:** The beak of these birds is flesh colored. When they reach breeding age, the tip of beak changes its color to a blackish, reddish or orange hue.

- **Gender identification:** The primary difference between male and female Gouldian Finches is the coloration. The females are less brightly colored in comparison to the males. Another feature that you can look out for is the coloration of the chest. The plumes on the chest have a bright purple color in the case of the males. The females, however, have chest feathers that are light mauve in color.

- **Description of juveniles:** The coloration of juvenile Gouldian Finches is quite distinctive. The side of the head, the neck and in some cases, the entire head is grey in color. The tail feathers, back and the wings are olive green in color.

The underside of the tail feathers are a pale brown color. The beaks have a red tip and are blackish overall. The feet and the legs are light brown in color.

When they hatch, Gouldian Finches do not have any feathering for about 12 days. They are pink in color until the feathers start to appear. Some young birds may even have distinctive blue structures on the sides of the beak. These structures have a sheen on them in order to help the parent birds locate the babies easily in the dark.

2. History of Gouldian Finches

The Gouldian Finch gets its name from the renowned ornithologist, John Gould. He named the bird after his wife and dedicated the discovery of this breathtaking bird to her. This is why the Gouldian Finch is also referred to as the Lady Gouldian quite often.

Originally, these birds were found across most parts of Northern Australia. Their habitat ranged from west Kimberley to the Cape of York Peninsula in Queensland that lies in the east.

Once considered a common backyard bird, these birds have quickly declined in number because of habitat loss and outbreak of diseases. Today, Gouldian Finches are considered endangered, as there are only about 2500 birds of breeding age in the wild.

These birds inhabit Western and Northern Australia in small populations. Sadly, these birds are now rare in Queensland.

These birds were discovered and recorded for the first time by John Gould in the year 1838. He described the bird for the first time and classified it under the *Amadina gouldiae* genus. His wife was the first one to lithograph these birds.

Although John Gould is credited for the discovery of these birds, they were classified a lot earlier as *'Poephile admirable'* by Jacques Bernard Homborn and Honroe Jacquinot in the year 1841. However, neither of them described the three Black Headed Gouldian Finches that they found. As a result, John Gould classified them again three years later.

In the year 1962, the birds were reclassified under the genus *Chloebia.* This is because almost 130 comprehensive families of these birds were found. This classification was specific to the Gouldian Finch.

The Yellow Headed Gouldian was found for the first time in the year 1876 by W.G Armit. They were found near Georgetown in North Queensland.

The first ever successful breeding program for Gouldian Finches was developed by Dr. E.P Ramsay in the year 1886. Following this, the first ever specimens of the Black Headed and Red Headed Gouldian Finches were imported into Europe in the year 1887.

In England, Reginald Philips was the first successful breeder of these beautiful birds. He was also the first person to prove that all three types of Finches, Red Headed, Yellow Headed and Black Headed came from the same species. He presented his research in the year 1891.

Finches became increasingly popular in Europe after they were exhibited for the first time ever in Berlin, Germany. After this, the Yellow Headed species was imported to Europe in the year 1936.

Meanwhile, breeding programs across the world had begun to produce hybrid varieties of these birds. Mutations such as Lutinos also began to be produced. The first Lutino Gouldian was wild caught by Hans Catt in Sydney, Australia around 1930. However, all these birds had very poor eyesight.

In the year 1936, the first ever hybrid was produced by K. Kleieidan in Germany. This hybrid was between a Gouldian Finch and a Blue faced Parrot Finch. The hybrids were later sold to the Zoological Museum in Copenhagen.

One of the most historic events in the timeline of Gouldian Finches is the ban on export of these birds from Australia. The Australian government laid down strict laws about exporting these birds and also breeding them in captivity. The diminishing numbers of these birds were responsible for the imposition of these laws.

However, the birds continued to be exported to various parts of the world by breeders in Europe. The first ever report of Lutino Gouldian Finches in Japan in the year 1960 was proof that these birds had also made their way into Asia. There were also reports of white breasted varieties of these birds in South Africa soon after in the year 1962.

These birds were also exported to USA and other parts of the world, making them a global favorite among bird lovers. These birds were sent to the US from Australia as well until the ban was imposed. Although the reports of Japanese Gouldians were only made in the year 1960, research shows that a lucrative Gouldian export business was already thriving in the 1930s. Most birds that were bred in Japan were sent to the United States.

It was in the year 1970 that Europe, primarily the western region, emerged as the biggest supplier of the Gouldian Finch in the American Market. The birds bred in Europe are considered the true predecessors of the original Australian Gouldians.

Sadly, these birds are bred in very unethical conditions in Europe. Most birds that are exported from Europe are from small scale breeders in Belgium and Holland. The advantage with these breeders is that they were able to match the demand of the American market for the Gouldian Finches.

This was done by collecting birds from several aviaries to match the required numbers. As a result, diseases among the birds also became common as they came from different, often poorly researched, environments.

The birds were also transported in poor conditions with boxes containing up to 100 birds at one time. This led to the birds arriving in a poor condition, leading to a popular belief that Gouldians as a species is an extremely delicate bird.

Today, however, the birds that are found in the US market are produced by local breeders. Japanese and European imports are very sparse because of the inhumane treatment of these birds in the process.

These birds are among the most popular and well established Finches in captivity. The demand remains high because of the coloration and the beautiful singing voices of these birds. However, if you plan to bring home one of these birds, make sure that you only buy from breeders after a thorough check and ensuring that no inhumane practices are involved. We will discuss this in detail in the following chapters.

3. Natural Habitat and Range
The natural range of the Gouldian Finch extends from the northern region of Australia and extends to the south until the 19 degree south latitude.

These birds require a variety of landscape options in order to survive. For instance, they need areas that have dense vegetation and hills. They also need areas that have grass undergrowth. This wide range of habitat is the result of the nesting requirements of the birds.

The other requirements for these birds to thrive include streams and rivers which are natural barriers. These water bodies are also responsible for the availability of food for these birds. They mainly feed on grass seeds.

In addition to this they also need the grass undergrowth of the woodland areas. In the wet season, the grass seeds are generally scarce. As a result, they need an alternative source. Usually, Gouldian Finches live in areas that are not very heavily populated.

It is common to find Goudian Finches near the eucalypt savannah. They generally avoid any wooded areas that are dense. These birds are not found in the tropical forests that span across the Cape York Peninsula.

The area that these birds populate is usually very hot. The maximum temperature in the natural habitat of these birds goes up to 40 degrees. During the rainy season, the temperature is usually around 30 degrees. These areas rarely have temperatures below 20 degrees.

In the southern parts of the habitat of Gouldian Finches, the temperature is lower in comparison to the northern parts. Here, the temperature is an average of 22 degrees. These high temperatures are another reason why these birds look for a habitat near water sources.

4. Types of Gouldian Finches
There are three primary types of Finches that are classified based on the color of the feathers on the head. There are several other mutations that these birds can be classified on the basis of.

a. Classification based on head color
The three different head colorations are most commonly found in the wild. As a result, for quite some time, these were believed to be the only three varieties of Gouldian Finches. The three types include:

1. **The Black Headed Gouldian**
   These birds get their name from the black coloration on the head. These birds are more common than any other type of Gouldian Finch in the wild. They are three times more common than the Red Headed Gouldian Finch. The black coloration of the feathers can be seen on the cheeks, head and the forehead.

2. **Yellow Headed Gouldian**
   The difference between the Black and Yellow Headed Gouldian Finches is that the latter has yellow markings on the cheek, head and near the eyes. These are the rarest of the three varieties of Finches found in the wild. The ratio of Yellow Headed Gouldians to Red and Black Gouldians is 1:3000. There are different shades of yellow coloration on the head of these birds. The color can vary from bright yellow to reddish orange in the case of males and from medium yellow to a brownish color in the females.

3. **Red Headed Finches**
   One fourth of the wild population of Finches consist of Red Headed Finches. These birds have red coloration on the cheeks, head and near the eyes. In the case of a mature adult male bird, the head is entirely red in color sometimes. However, in the case of females the red coloration is interspersed with dark feathers. This was believed to be the result of a cross between Red and Black Gouldians. However, the reason for this split coloration is that the gene responsible for the red coloration does not split in females.

b. Classification based on mutation
Over the years cross breeding in the wild and in captivity have lead to hybrids. These experiments have also led to several mutations that have resulted in some of the most brilliant colors on the bodies of these Finches. The different mutations are as follows:

1. **Green**
   This mutation occurs even when one of the parents shows these colors. The back of the bird contains rich green feathers in males while the females have a duller hue. The breast of the male is bright purple while females have a lighter

coloration. The belly is a rich yellow color in males and pale yellow in females. Sometimes, the males may also have a bright orange line running between the breast and the belly. The head can be orange, black or red.

There is a turquoise blue band just behind the head. A jet black line separates this band from the head. The birds have beaks that have a yellow or red tip.

2. **Blue**

   For this mutation to occur, both parents should exhibit the mutation. With the blue mutation, all the green feathers on the body are replaced by blue feathers. The ones that are orange or red are replaced by beige feathers. Even the ones that are yellow, particularly on the belly, are beige or cream in color.

3. **Seagreen**

   The origin of this coloration is unknown. These birds are considered to be partial Blue Gouldians. It is also believed that the coloration was the result of certain environmental conditions. The green feathers on the body are replaced by a mixture of green and blue feathers. The intensity of the red, orange and yellow feathers is less, making them look paler.

4. **Pastel**

   The male and female birds look quite different from one another. In this type of mutation, any back color, be it blue, green or others, is diluted to make the color appear pastel. The black marking are also replaced by grey or white markings.

5. **Dilute**

   This mutation occurs when both the parents have the same mutation. These birds are generally yellow-green or light lime green in color. The breast and the belly coloration is the same as other finches, purple and yellow respectively. The black colorations and markings are usually grey or pale grey. The blue markings are very pale in color.

5. Gouldian Finch behavior

Gouldian Finches have specific behavior patterns that make them rather unique. One uncanny quality of these birds is that they tend to drink water by drawing it. They consume a lot more water in comparison to their body weight. These birds need water on a daily basis which makes them choose habitats that are near water bodies.

They will inhabit shallow waterholes that are generally clear of predators. Gouldian Finches prefer to stay away from any human inhabitation. However, these birds are social within flocks and usually live in large colonies.

In comparison to other birds that eat seeds, these birds have quite a unique diet. They consume seeds of annual grass varieties such as Vacoparis and Sorghum. These seeds are available when the birds are molting. These seeds are more nutritious in comparison to the seeds of perennial grasses like Spinifex.

Gum trees and Eucalyptus trees form an important part of these birds' habitat. Salmon gum and white gum trees that grow further north are preferred by these birds. These trees have cavities that are used as nests by these birds. They usually build their nests in cavities that have been abandoned by other birds like budgerigars or other varieties of Parrots. These birds may also build nests in tall grasses or in shrubs at times.

Gouldian Finches have very complex social instincts. There is also a shortage of appropriate nesting areas. So, you will normally find more than one pair sharing a nest and raising the hatchlings there.

The nesting season for birds in the wild begins in the later part of the rainy season. During this time, these birds produce large amounts of sex hormones. This encourages mates to find them and the pair begins to look for nesting options. The breeding season overlaps with the season when food is available for the birds in abundance. That way, by the time the offspring reaches the molting season which is in the next wet season, they will have several food options such as local grass and fresh seeds.

The rainy season in the areas inhabited by Gouldian fluctuates quite a bit. As a result, these birds exhibit a certain type of behavior that is also called opportunistic breeding or nesting. This helps the birds adapt to the different climatic conditions.

In case of the dry years, these birds have a nesting season that is shorter. Then, they may have a single nesting or two at the most. During the years when the rainfall is ample, these birds have a lot of food at their disposal. This leads to a longer nesting season. The birds will nest two to three times during a good year.

In the nesting season, the average temperature during the day time is about 33 degrees and is about 19 degrees at night.

In order to adjust to the climatic conditions, these birds also exhibit rapid molting. The chicks reach adolescence quite early, sometimes as early as 2 months. However, in some weather conditions, the birds are under a lot of stress which may delay this process. The birds are at maximum stress between the end and beginning of each wet season. This is when food sources are scanty.

Rapid molting is an evolutionary adaptation process. Since the tropical forests have very unpredictable weather conditions, it is essential that the birds complete the molting process before the bad weather sets in. As a result, the molting process speeds up. This gives the birds ample time to migrate to areas that have the necessary conditions for the birds to thrive.

In case of events like extreme cold weather or a sudden lack of food, these birds interrupt the molting process and retain the youth feathers. This allows them to be mobile even when the feathers are not completely developed.

Rapid molting is one of the most remarkable traits of this bird. In the wild, molting occurs in young birds as well as in adults between September and November. Usually the molting process is complete by mid-December. Sometimes, it may end as early as October or November, depending upon the weather conditions available.

6. Conservation status
Over the years the wild populations of these birds have diminished quite significantly. Today, some populations have been washed out completely, leaving a few thousand Gouldian Finches in the wild.

In fact, the Australian government is taking several measures to restore the numbers of these birds. Human civilization is one of the biggest causes for the decline in the numbers of these birds. There are several other causal factors as well, such as:

- **Parasites:** During the 1980's, research revealed the presence of several air sac mites in the wild populations of Finches. These parasites led to the outbreak of several diseases that quickly washed out large populations of the birds.

- **Trapping:** Gouldian Finches are a great source of income because of their increasing demand in the pet market. Bird traps had been used extensively between 1960 and 1988, which led to the capture of thousands of these birds purely for breeding. However, since these birds are able to reproduce fast, the populations were restored. However other factors along with trapping led to their quick decline.

- **Field Burning:** The aborigines usually burn small patches of land to clear them out for other uses. There is a lot of advancement in the technology used to burn the fields. With the burning of fields, the food of the Finches was also destroyed. This included seeds and grass that the birds need in order to survive.

- **Grazing:** Extensive grazing, especially in the dry season, leaves these birds with no food to consume. Cattle generally graze on the perennial grasses can be associated with the decline in the population of these birds. The Australian government recommended fencing areas in these grasslands specifically for grazing. However, the belief that this may affect the productivity of cattle has not allowed this plan to materialize.

With the ban in export and also strict laws about the care of wild Gouldian Finches, the numbers have been significantly restored. These birds do reproduce fast, which allows the numbers to be restored   naturally   as   well.

Chapter 2: Popular Gouldian Finch Myths

If you are planning to bring home a Gouldian Finch, there are chances that you have heard of many myths surrounding these birds. Most wives tales that you have heard about these birds can affect the care that you provide. So, it is essential that you equip yourself with the right information.

This chapter helps you learn the truth about these birds and also understand where these myths originated from.

1. Nests are required for these birds to rest
This is easily one of the most common myths about Gouldian Finches. Most people believe that not providing a nest all year long might even harm the bird.

The truth is that nests are essential when the breeding season begins. In the wild, Gouldian Finches build nests in order to find a mate and start breeding. Once the eggs are laid and the baby birds fledge, the parents and the babies move to a new place. They leave the nest behind or it might be used by other species of birds. Eventually, this nest falls apart over time.

Gouldian Finches use nests only for about 2 months every year. For the next 10 months, these birds use a perch to rest on. They use shrubs, trees and even rooftops of houses as resting areas. They need a space that is slightly closed in order to rest.

When a nest is available, the egg laying instincts of the female bird kicks in. Having a nest all year along might lead to one clutch every month. However, in the wild, these birds do not lay more than 3 clutches all year long. In fact, there are years when these birds have only one clutch per year.

In the case of the male, the protective instinct kicks in when you provide a nest all year along. In the wild, after the eggs are laid, even the female becomes protective about the nest. They share the duties of incubating the eggs. Finches can become aggressive when they

17

are protecting their nest. For this reason, there may be fights among the birds if you have a flock in your home. One pair attacks the other and this aggression only gets worse eventually. Since they are housed in the aviary, you are not even able to separate the pairs.

In order to reduce any aggression and to make sure that your birds have a normal breeding cycle, using a nest only in the breeding season is a must.

2. The female only lays eggs when housed with a male
With Finches, you will see that the female can lay eggs even when a male is not housed with her. The egg laying is a regular cycle with female Finches and it is a sign that she is healthy. However, when she has no male companion, the rate at which the eggs are laid will reduce. With even a single, healthy female, you may find eggs in the cage from time to time.

In case you house a pair together, they will produce about 3 clutches every year. If the female does not produce any eggs all year long or lays many eggs even when she is housed alone, there are chances that the diet is inadequate or that her environment is not conducive.

3. It is alright for Finches to breed anytime of the year
If your Finches are laying eggs and producing young ones randomly over the year, then it is harmful not only to their health but also to the health of the young ones. Generally, Finches tend to breed readily. After successfully raising offspring for the first time, they will continue to lay one clutch after another. The process of parenting can be so stressful for the birds that it could also become fatal.

It is best that you remove the nest from the cage after the offspring have fledged. You can put it back in the next breeding season to keep them healthy.

4. Finches can die from loneliness
Finches thrive best when they are kept in flocks or as pairs. However, when provided with healthy living conditions, these birds can thrive alone if they are not housed with a companion.

That said, since these birds need a companion of their kind, they can be under stress when they are housed alone. However, unless the environment that they live in undergoes a sudden change or if there is an outbreak of some infection, chances are that the bird will still survive.

In cases when the Finch dies after the companion dies or is removed, there are other causal factors that are usually responsible for the bird's death.

5. They only breed with birds their own age

If the bird has a potential mate who is capable of attracting the opposite sex and can prove that he or she can provide for the nest, age is not an important factor. What matters is that the birds should be healthy. One common reason for the origin of this myth is that as the Finch ages, he or she is not considered a potential mate by a younger bird. This is only because the ability to rear chicks may diminish as the bird ages. However, if the bird is healthy, breeding is not an issue. If you introduce a bird who is better in health and overall condition, chances are that he or she will be picked as the more suitable mate. This can also lead to an existing pair splitting.

6. Finches can thrive only on seeds

This is not true for any pet bird. Birds need a variety of food choices in order for them to be healthy. We will discuss the diet of the bird in detail in the following chapters. However, you need to remember that an all seed diet is not good enough for your Finch.

7. Finches are only decorative birds

If you are looking for a cuddly pet, then you may easily believe this myth. However, even though these birds are not as interactive as Parrots, they make wonderful pets. They are extremely fun to watch as they play around in their cages. In addition to that, the voice of these birds is very soothing and pleasant.

8. Finches are extremely fragile

Most often, people who bring home Finches do not understand the requirements of the bird. Even if you have raised Parrots or other birds before, you need to make sure that you do your research to provide for specific species of birds.

Most often, finches die because of improper care. If you are able to provide them with a good environment, they will thrive. That said, you also need to make sure that the genetics of your bird are strong. That is achieved by finding a breeder who uses ethical and healthy breeding practices. If you buy from breeders who do not follow necessary standards, you may be bringing home a bird that is already sick. Naturally, your bird will not survive even with the best care conditions.

9. Finches can be tamed by clipping their wings

In the case of Finches it is recommended that you never clip their wings. First, since these birds are not as interactive as Parrots, they would be spending most of their time in the cage. Even if you do take the bird out of the cage from time to time to provide basic training, it is not recommended to clip the wings.

The only way you can tame a Gouldian Finch is by hand raising. This is not an easy process, however. Baby Finches are extremely delicate and need to be handled carefully.

The reason why you can clip the wings of birds like Parrots and not that of Finches is very simple. With Parrots, the beaks and feet are quite strong. That allows the bird to move around the cage or climb and stay active even when the wings are clipped. However, with Finches, movement becomes impossible when the wings are clipped. Even when they hop, these birds use the assistance of their wings. Clipping the wings may also mean that the bird is unable to get away from any fights or may even be unable to get to the food and water bowls when needed. This can be fatal to the bird.

Chapter 3: Sourcing Gouldian Finches

The source of your Gouldian Finch is extremely important. Making sure that you purchase your bird from a reliable source ensures that the bird is healthy and will thrive better.

There are several unethical breeding practices that lead to unhealthy birds that not only have very few chances of survival but may also spread diseases in your existing flock.

There are different ways to look for the right source for your Gouldian Finch. This chapter also gives you simple tips to check your source and make sure that it is reliable.

1. Best places to get a Finch from
Be careful where you bring your birds from. You must always do your research before you actually pick a Finch or a pair of Finches. There are various options that people can suggest to you with respect to buying a bird. There are advertisements that are frequent, too. However, you must never blindly opt for something. There are chances that you will bring home a bird that is poor in health or has developed some behavioral issues due to poor care.

Buying from a pet store
A pet store has to be the most convenient option available for a new Finch owner. You can walk up to any local pet store and check out the conditions that the birds are being raised in. If you notice that the cages are dirty and that their feeders and water baths are messy, it is a first sign that the bird has been raised under poor conditions. You must also ask the pet store owners questions about the species of Finches and about the care that you need to provide. If they are able to answer confidently, then it is possible that they have enough experience with these birds. Pet stores that have a good ambience for the birds to grow in will be a little more expensive. But, that is always worth it.

Buying from a breeder

There are two kinds of breeders, irrespective of the type of pet you plan to bring home. You have backyard breeders who are doing it solely for their passion towards the birds and you have commercial breeders who are in it for the money. The latter do not stick to breeding ethics, affecting the health of the birds. When you are buying from a breeder, make sure that you visit the premises to check the breeding area, the coops and the baby areas. If you feel like they have been maintained well, you can make a commitment. If not, there are chances that your bird is not in the best health. Ask the breeder to help you connect with previous clients to get feedback on the health of their birds. Normally a breeder will not hesitate if he is sure of the quality of the birds he is trying to sell to you.

Approaching rescue groups

This is a good idea if you have some experience with raising birds. There are several rescue groups that will bring in abandoned, injured or even abused birds. These birds are usually rehabilitated first before they are sent into a new home. Adopting from a rescue group is a great idea as it is a noble thing to do. Besides that, you will not have to spend anything on the bird. Now, what you need to understand is that birds in such shelters may have developed behavioral problems or may require medical attention. Only when you are prepared to provide this care should you bring a bird home. If you do not have the experience yourself, you must at least have someone who can give you good advice and support you.

Buying online

This is the least preferred option. Unless you are looking for a specific type of Finch, you may not want to choose online buying. There are several reliable sources too. If you can connect with a client who has already made a satisfactory purchase, you may order your bird online. However, remember that birds undergo a lot of stress when they are shipped or transported. This can make the housebreaking process a little challenging. You must also make sure that you go over the terms and conditions several times before you actually commit to an online store. They should be able to give you a refund or an exchange if the health of your bird deteriorates in a given period of time. Check for the shipping conditions that they have on their website as well.

2. Making a good choice

There are several obvious signs that help you identify whether you are making a good purchase or not. Here are some things that you need to look out for whether you are buying your Finch from a breeder or a pet store:

- If they are offering the birds at very low prices, it means that something is amiss. They could be smuggled or may be really unwell.

- If the aviaries or the cages are messy and unkempt, the birds are most likely to be of poor health.

- If your breeder or pet store cannot give you any information about the bird that you can verify, they are probably not experienced enough.

- If you notice that the aviaries are overcrowded, the birds may have behavioral issues like aggression. Usually, Finches do not thrive well when there are too many birds in one small enclosure.

- There are obvious physical defects that you need to be careful about.

- If the birds are not alert when you approach the cage, it is cause for concern.

3. How to identify healthy birds

The first sign of good health is the posture of the bird. A healthy Finch will be erect in its posture. They will also be alert to the slightest sounds and actions. They have a very clear look in the eyes that makes them appear sharp and intelligent. The feathers are tight with no bald spots. When in an aviary, no other bird besides the mate is allowed to peck the bird.

How to examine a bird

Most breeders and pet store owners will let you examine the birds. Make sure you wear soft gloves because a bird that is not used to you will peck and bite. Take a good look at the bird all the way from the tip of the beak to the tail. Here are the signs of good health:

- The beak should be able to close fully. It must be smooth all over the surface.

- The head should not have any bald spot. Unless the bird is molting, bald spots indicate poor health and breeding conditions.

- The wings should not have any broken shafts in them.

- You must examine each leg of the bird, separately. The toes should be straight with all the nails. There should not be any broken nails. In males, especially, toenails are extremely important. If you want to buy a pair of Finches that you may breed in the future, a male without toenails is a problem. His poor grip will not help him mate properly.

- The tail must be neat and clean.

- Feel the breastbone of the bird. It usually extends from the middle of the breast to the bottom. On the either side of this bone, the flesh must feel firm.

- The cloaca or the anus of the bird must be examined. If you find sticky substances or any dirt in this area, it is an indication of possible intestinal problems.

- Breathing should be even. If you hear any peculiar sounds, like a squeak in the breathing, it indicates a respiratory problem in the bird.

- Lastly, blow on the feathers of the chest and the stomach gently. If you see that the skin is healthy, it means that the bird is healthy. On the other hand, if you notice any redness or blotching, it is the sign of skin problems or infections.

Now, any bird that has one or more of the above problems, does not mean that he or she will die quickly. There are several health issues that can be cured with minimum care. So, if the breeder or the pet store has been recommended by a friend or family, don't just dismiss them when you see any of the signs mentioned above. Tell your breeder and have the bird examined by a vet. It may not be a good idea to invest in a bird knowing that it is in trouble. However, if your breeder can guarantee recovery, it is a good idea to consider it. If the breeder has been recommended by several bird owners, he will be a great support for you in the future.

Birds that come with health issues need a lot of care. They may also be poor breeders. So, if you want to breed your birds, make sure that you pick the best quality stock.

4. Health certificates for birds

Getting a health certificate for a pet bird is mandatory. This is a guarantee of sorts on the health and quality of the bird that you are bringing home. For Finches, your health guarantee is valid for a 90 day period. In that time, if the health of your bird deteriorates, the breeder will give you a replacement or will return your money. Any breeder who practices good husbandry will give you a health certificate by default. If he or she hesitates, you may want to reconsider your options.

Note: If you are ordering a bird online, you may not be able to avail a health certificate. This is because the health problems may be caused due to the shipping conditions that the breeder has no control over.

Here are a few conditions that you will see in any bird health certificate:

- The bird should be checked for any health issues within 72 hours of the purchase. Usually, you need to consult a vet recommended by the aviary. However, if you can find a breeder who lets you choose the vet, it is a better idea, as you can be sure of no internal connections.

- If any illness is caused because of poor conditions that you keep the birds in, the health guarantee will not cover for it.

- Accidents are not covered by the health insurance. This includes any attack by your existing pets, fires, smoke etc.
- No veterinarian costs will be covered by a health insurance.

- Behavioral issues in the birds will not be covered in this insurance.

- In the case of Finches, any incompatibility between the birds will be covered in this insurance in case you are buying them in pairs. This is especially true when you are investing in a bird that is expensive.

When you get your birds examined, if the vet is able to determine the presence of any health condition that may be bacterial, viral or genetic, the breeder must give you a replacement.

For first time bird owners, it is a good idea to consult a friend who already owns a bird with respect to the conditions mentioned in the agreement. Normally, there are aviculturists who will offer this service at a small price. If you have no experience with Finches, this is a good option for you. They will not only be able to verify the terms and conditions but also the health of the bird that you are bringing home.

5. Getting a second hand bird

You may have the opportunity of bringing home the pet from another home and becoming a foster parent. This may happen when someone decides to move and is unable to take their pet along with them. They may be unable to meet the demands of a bird due to personal or professional reasons. If this is the source that you are opting for, you may want to learn a few things first.

You can bring the bird home from a rescue home or from the home of a friend or family. Usually, any bird that has been abandoned by the owner will be sent off to a shelter. Now, when you choose this bird, you need to go into every detail of its history. This includes the caging practices, the history of the bird's relationship with the previous owner, the habits that the bird is used to such as having a blanket over the cage, diet, sex etc. The more you know, the more you can understand about the possible behavior of the bird. These experiences will have a very strong impact on the personality of the bird.

The first thing to know about a Finch that you are adopting is that you have to keep your expectations really low. They may not form a bond with you instantly or may not form a bond at all. Remember that this bird has undergone the stress of changing homes, forming new bonds and in worst cases, abuse. This may be very annoying for someone who is expecting to have a loving bird that will play and cuddle. If you can prepare yourself to provide care for the bird despite possible behavioral issues, you must bring home a second hand bird. Otherwise, you may give up on the bird, adding to his existing stress and plight.

If you are planning to adopt a Finch, here are a few helpful tips for you:

- Make sure that you have some previous experience with respect to dealing with birds.

- You need to be able to understand the difference between a bird who is young and a bird who is mature. The former is likely to have a more volatile personality. They will respond to everything differently, including food.

- You must be willing to spend a certain amount of money on professional care for the bird. If you are a first time owner, this is a must. Do not pretend to know anything about the bird if you really don't. That is in the best interest of your feathery friend.

- You need to be very patient and persistent. If you walk out on the bird, you will make his condition worse. Only if you are ready to deal with a challenge should you accept to adopt a bird.

On the bright side, with constant care, the behavioral issues of the bird will disappear with time if you are going to provide him or her with a loving home. The time that this will take is one thing that cannot be guaranteed. It is also possible that you may adopt a perfectly well behaved bird with no signs of a behavioral issue. It is harder when you bring home a bird that has formed a bond with the owner than when you bring home a bird that has been neglected or ill-treated. The latter is almost like a brand new bird that will adapt to your home in no time. The only thing you will have to do is love your bird with your heart and you will receive the same in return.

6. Cage or Aviary?

When you are dealing with a breeder, there are two possibilities: the birds are raised in a cage or they are raised in an aviary. Each practice has its own advantages and disadvantages. Depending upon what suits you better you may choose a breeder or pet store.

Cage reared birds

It is a good idea to buy birds that are reared in cages, especially if you are planning on bringing home a pair of Finches. The good thing is that the pairs of birds can be reared to have the same diet and similar habits. This gives the new owner clear specifications about taking care of the bird when he or she brings them home. Birds that are reared in cages are less prone to diseases and injury as there is very little aggression among pairs of Finches or lone Finches. The breeder or pet store owner is able to keep a close eye on these birds and will be able to tell if anything is wrong immediately. You can also control breeding and the progeny when you have birds in a cage.

On the flipside, these birds may be lazy as the space provided is not enough for them to fly around. In addition to that, they may develop other issues because they do not have the luxury of flight. Keeping pairs or individuals in cages can be really expensive. And, who will have to bear those costs ultimately? The buyer. So, when you choose a breeder who usually rears birds separately, you may have to bear some additional costs as well.

Aviary reared birds

If the breeder has a closed aviary concept where a lot of quarantining measures are taken before you introduce a new bird to the flock, you can opt for it. If not, there are chances that your bird has diseases or even behavioral problems such as aggression. However, when raised in aviaries, birds tend to be happier because they have a lot of space to fly around and play. These birds are more instinctive and have a behavior that is closer to the wild species. They can pick their own mates, which means that the bonds are a lot stronger.

However, with aviaries comes the risk of infections. Also, it is hard to tell which birds are the parents of the new borns. It is also hard to give these birds specialized diets as all the birds in the aviary will be given the same food to eat.

The choice really depends upon what type of behavior you are expecting from the Finches. If you want them to be more active, aviary raised birds are the better way to go. However, if you want to be able to raise the birds in a specific way and control their habits and diet, you need to choose birds that are reared in individual cages.

Birds that are raised in a cage are usually hand bred unlike the ones in an aviary. It is safe to say that hand bred birds are almost always more social and a lot easier to tame. Most bird owners prefer cage reared birds simply because they can be trained easily. This is possible with aviary bred birds only when you bring them home as a baby. Otherwise, they will display a lot of instinctive behavior that can be difficult to change or manage for beginners.

7. Baby bird or adult?

This is a common problem that new bird owners face. They are unsure if it is a good idea to bring home a sexually mature bird or a baby. Well, they both have their pros and cons. It is up to the owners to decide what kind of care they are willing to provide for the birds. Then, it is easier to choose between a baby and an adult. Here are the pros and cons of each:

Baby bird

Housebreaking is much easier with baby birds. These birds do not come with any baggage or behavioral issues. So, they are most likely to adapt to a new place faster. Most baby Finches require hand feeding for the first few days. So, if you are bringing a baby home, you need to learn how to handle them and feed them as well. It is also demanding in terms of time as babies need a lot more care.

With baby birds, you also have to understand that their bodies are extremely delicate. This means that you may injure the bird when you are handling it. In addition to that, any slack in care can lead to infections. You also have to deal with the problem of moulting at about 8 months of age. This is when the birds can be very irritable and nippy. It is almost like dealing with a human teen.

The biggest advantage of bringing a baby bird home is that you can teach them your ways easily. They come with an empty slate and will be able to pick up the exact behavior that you expect from them. You can regulate the eating habits, timings for food, socialization and several other factors.

Adult birds

You will call a bird an adult when it has become sexually mature. In the case of Finches, this can happen anytime between 8 and 12 months of age. Usually, an adult bird is trained to do a lot of things. So, that is a big responsibility that is lifted off your shoulders. Now, this also means that you will have to worry about the behavior that these birds come with. If they have any signs of aggression or depression, it will take you a lot of time to get rid of these problems.

When you bring an adult bird home, you have to remove him from an environment that he or she is used to. This can be extremely stressful for the birds. You can expect an aggravation in behavioral issues, if any. You at least need to prepare yourself to make the extra effort to help the bird get used to you and your home.

The advantage with adult birds is that they are easier to handle because they are well developed and not as weak as the babies. Health wise, you only have to worry about preexisting conditions. With the right care, they are less prone to infections and diseases in comparison to the baby birds.

8. Is your pet imported?

Some varieties of Finches may be legally imported to countries like the USA. They are brought in from Asia or Europe. Now, with imported birds, there are several guidelines that you must be fully aware of.

To begin with, these birds must be quarantined for a period of 30 days by a wing of the US department of Agriculture, called the Animal and Plant Health services. The birds will be kept in an isolated cage for this period and each one will be provided with a unique leg band to help you identify your pet. This is done to ensure that no disease or infection spreads within the country because of an imported bird. These birds will be given special medication prescribed by these authorities with ready access to food and water.

So, you can be assured that the health of your bird will be taken good care of.

These birds are also examined by specially appointed avian vets who need to confirm that the bird is not carrying any communicable disease that may affect poultry or people. If the bird is suspected of an infection, they are usually not allowed entry. If this is the case, you need to opt for having them sent back. If not, these birds are euthanized. You will have to bear the costs of sending the bird back home.

In case you have the slightest suspicion that a breeder or pet store owner is not importing the bird for you, but is smuggling it in, make sure that you avoid the purchase. Birds that have been smuggled into a country pose maximum threat. In fact, diseases like Newcastle disease that became an epidemic have been caused by exotic birds that were smuggled into the United States of America. Even if you obtain any information about smuggled birds, it is best to report it to the Customs office or any agriculture authority in your country. In the USA, you can contact the US Department of Agriculture for this.

If you want to purchase a Finch to start breeding, then an imported variety is not the best option. These birds are usually not ready for breeding and may not even breed when brought home in pairs. These birds are used to a very different environment, food and ambience. Hence, they may be severely stressed when they are imported.

There are special regulations with respect to the species of birds that you can bring home. Some of them will require a leg band at all times while others may be banned altogether. You must make sure that you are aware of all the legal considerations about bringing in a certain species of Finch into your home. In case you are unsure, you may contact avian vets, authorized government veterinary services or any import and export staff to confirm. Any doubt or hesitation must be dealt with immediately to ensure that you do not put the future of your pet at risk.

9. Transporting the bird home

The next consideration after you have finalized the bird and cleared all the legal concerns is actually bringing it home. Most often, the pet store or the breeder will give you a small cage or a box to carry your pet in. Enquire about this before you go over to pick up your pet. If they are not going to provide any cage, you can carry a box or a cat carrier if you have one. If not, you can buy transport cages. This, however, is an unwanted expense that you can avoid.

If your Finch has been imported, it means that the bird is severely stressed already because of the customs, a change in the food and water quality, strange noises etc. Then, when they are put in a travelling cage, the stress just builds. There is a mild amount of stress even with the locally bred birds. When you are driving the bird home, you only make this stress a little worse.

The bird will be a little shaken up because of the ride and there are chances that the body temperature will shoot up. So, make sure that you keep the cage away from sunlight and also keep the air-conditioning on in your vehicle at all times. That said, these birds do not do well with any draft either. So, that should be avoided too.

In case you are travelling in winter, you need to wrap the cage with a blanket, making a few ventilation holes. You also need to provide seeds and water for the bird.

If you are making a long trip home, say about 6-8 hours, you need to take a break every three hours. This break should at least be 20 minutes long. These 20 minute breaks will help the bird eat and actually recover from the bumpy ride.

Avoid music and talking when you are bringing the bird home. These are all new sounds that will only stress the bird out more. It is also a good idea for just one person from the family to go any pick the bird up. That way, you can be sure that the ride is not noisy. If you have children, especially, avoid taking them along if they are too little. It is natural for the little ones to be excited about the new pet. They will want to look at it and play with it. But, that is a terrible experience for your bird.

10. Single bird or multiple birds?
Finches are not too friendly with human beings. They are social birds that prefer their own kind for the most part. So, if you are planning to bring home Gouldian Finches, you must think of a flock or at least a pair.

Single birds, unlike popular belief, will not die. However, they show signs of loneliness by vocalizing too much. They even display behavioral issues such as feather plucking. Although a single bird will give its owner more attention, he or she becomes extremely lonely over time.

It is best that you buy these birds in pairs. One male and one female is the best option as they will usually become mates for life. Ask the breeder or the pet store for a pair that has already bonded. If you are introducing a companion to your Finch, you can follow the guidelines mentioned in the following chapters.

If you are worried about egg laying, all you need to make sure is remove the nest from the cage. Without the right nesting conditions, these birds are less likely to breed.

If you want to keep multiple birds, choosing birds of the same species is best. However, Gouldian Finches are known to be the mildest among all the types of Finches. So, you can even mix them with other species.

Make sure that your flock contains at least three pairs. If you do not pair the birds, there may be aggression as the birds attempt to find a suitable mate during the breeding season. Make sure that your birds have ample space to avoid any confrontation or fights. One pair of Gouldian Finches requires a cage that is at least 20 inches high and 28 inches long.

You can also pair birds of the same gender. If this is your preference, having two females is better than having two males in a cage. The latter may lead to dominance related fights. The vocalization helps you tell the birds apart. If the birds are singing, they are most likely male. Female Gouldian Finches rarely vocalize and may only chirp or make beeping sounds.

Chapter 4: Top 5 Care Requirements of Gouldian Finches

Proper care is a must when you bring your bird home. Make sure that you keep these 5 requirements of the bird in mind if you have decided to bring a Gouldian Finch home.

1. Housing

Since the bird will be spending most of its waking hours in his or her enclosure, you need to make sure that the bird feels comfortable in that space. The first thing to consider is the size and shape of the enclosure. The rule of the thumb is never get round cages. This is because the round ones do not provide any place for the bird to retreat in. They must either be square or rectangular. The ideal size for a pair of birds is about 28 inches horizontally and 20 inches vertically. If you are housing two Finches at a time, make sure that they are both able to comfortably spread their wings without bumping into one another when the fly. Here are some pointers that will help you pick the perfect enclosure for your bird:

- Finches love to chew. So you need to make sure that the frame of the cage is sturdy. It is recommended that you get a powder coated cage or one that is made from stainless steel.

- Finches cannot withstand cold. If the enclosure of your bird is subject to any sort of draft or wind, you can install a wind block in the cage to keep your bird protected.

- You will need at least two perches to keep your Finch healthy and active. Now, make sure that you purchase these perches from pet shops. If you try to make or build these perches, you need to make sure that the type of wood that you use is not poisonous or dangerous for the bird. One such type of wood is oleander.

- The enclosure must be protected from common predators like mice, rats and snakes. There may be other types of pests like opossums and squirrels that will not exactly feed on the birds. However, they may carry several infectious diseases. Therefore you need a sturdy enclosure.

- You need to provide your Finches with ample water. If you live in an area with hot weather, you need to be extra careful about providing enough water for your bird.

- The length of the cage is more important than the height. This will give your pet room for exercise and movement. For birds that are as active as Finches, space is one of the most important factors to ensure that they are healthy and happy.

- The spacing between the bars should be such that the bird is unable to put his head through. In the case of Finches, the bars should also be thick enough to bear the dismantling attempts that the bird will make on the bars.

- The cage should be portable. So, if you want to take your bird out into the garden or if you have to move for whatever reason, you should be able to shift the cage easily. Some Finch owners also move the cage around to a different room at night. Then, the cage needs to be extremely convenient. It should fit easily through doors and if it has wheels, they should be of great quality.

Preparing the cage
The first thing to do would be to make sure that there are no traces of zinc and lead. If you purchase a non-coated metal cage, you must wash it with vinegar water with 1 part vinegar and 2 parts water. You need to do this frequently if the cage is kept outdoors. That way, any new deposits of zinc will be removed.

Touch all the bars and surfaces of the cage to make sure that there are no sharp edges. In case you see any spots without paint, you need to wash it well to remove metal fillings. It is advisable to wash a cage with high pressure water if you buy it from a pet store with other birds. That way, you will be able to get rid of any possible feather dander on the cage that may cause infections to your bird.

Food and water bowls

The number one rule with feeders and water bowls is that they must never be placed just below the perch to avoid any droppings in it. If you choose hooded feeders, make sure that they are large enough for the bird to eat from. If not, it will only add to the mess.

Water dispensers will keep the water free from droppings but they wont let the bird bathe and preen. This is a very important part of the bird's routine. In addition to that, these dispensers are pretty hard to clean. If you have two water bowls, place one near the food and one away from it. If you have just one water bowl, place it at the opposite end of the cage from the food bowl to encourage the birds to exercise.

If you have more than one bird housed in a cage, they need individual food bowls. That will make sure that there is peace among the birds. If not, you will often see them challenging each other. Foraging is an important activity for Finches. That will keep their beaks trimmed and clean. So, add a few foraging toys in the cage and place some food in them. It is better to put treats into foraging toys. You can even scrunch up paper with treats and leave it on the floor if the cage. The birds will love the challenge of finding their treats. This is a wonderful activity to improve the mental health of your bird.

Adding perches

Finches require perches. They in fact, need two or more of them to feel at home. When selecting perches, make sure that you avoid the plastic ones. These can be flimsy and uneven. It causes a great deal of irritation for the bird's feet. A better option is a natural perch that you can get from any pet store. These can be made at home or purchased at a store.

If you plan to make a natural perch, check if the wood you are using is safe for the birds. Next, you will have to measure the perch that you will be using for your bird. There are many sources for natural perches; you can find them in your own garden, the park or even your neighbor's garden. Make sure that you do not pick up your piece of wood from areas close to the street. They may be polluted. Whatever you bring home, inspect it well. There should be no droppings from wild birds. The foliage and leaves should be trimmed off well and the branch should be washed and dried. These natural perches have a good texture that lets your bird sit comfortably. It also helps the bird exercise his feet and beak.

There are special concrete perches that you can buy from local pet stores. These perches are great for the birds to keep their toe nails and their beaks trimmed. Some people may recommend that you use sandpaper covers on these perches to keep the nails trim. This is not the best option as it will cause bumblefoot in birds who have a vitamin A deficiency. These types of perches are known as conditioning perches.

Sleeping perches
Finches need an additional perch to sleep on. You need to place this perch on the highest possible point in the cage. This perch should be placed on the side of the cage against the wall. You can also try small tents like the "Happy Hut" that other varieties of Parrots like the Lorikeets and Conures really love to rest in.

Placing the perch
The common mistake that most people make with a perch is placing it right in the middle of the cage. If you have two birds, you can place the perches parallel to one another. Sometimes, they may just share the same perch. You can observe them and make necessary changes. It is best that you place the toys along the edges of the cage. If you place toys like swings right over the perches, there are chances that the bird will fracture a wing while trying to stretch. Placing toys too close to a perch is also dangerous because any movement of the wings due to fright or agitation will result in broken feathers.

You can decide how many perches you want to place inside the cage depending upon how much space your bird has. Finches will fly around the cage. So, unless you have enough space, do not add more than two perches at a time. There must be enough head and tail space for the bird. This means that the roof and the floor should be at a good distance from the perch to ensure that the birds don't have to curl up or crouch down. Even the sides should be away from the cage to avoid any damage caused to the feathers due to constant rubbing.

2. Diet

As mentioned before, simply giving your bird seeds will not fulfil his nutritional requirements.

In this section we will discuss the several options that you have with respect to feeding your Finches. The pros and cons of each type of food will be discussed in detail to help you make the best choice for your birds.

Bird seeds

You have a host of different types of bird seeds that you can get. The best type of seeds to buy, if you choose to feed your bird seeds, is the premixed variety. If you are experienced with birds you can, of course, make your own mix. That way you can customize it as per the requirement of your birds.

In case you opt for a premixed seed bag, it is a good idea to pick up the special Finch bags. That ensures that the seeds aren't too large for your bird.

Seeds should always be fresh. You should make sure that there are no droppings of rodents or cobwebs in your seed bag. Bugs and larvae are the main issue when it comes to bird seeds.

The best way to judge is to smell the bag of seeds. In case it smells rancid, discard it right away. You can also apply a simple towel test to the seeds. You can fold a spoonful of seeds in paper and moisten it a little. In case of fresh seeds, they will sprout. If the seeds are stale or dead, you will not see any signs of sprouts.

Millet spray is a type of seed that your Finches will simply adore. The seeds are still present on the stalk and it is a great pass time for the birds to pull these seeds out and eat them up.

It is best that you reserve seeds for treats, especially millet spray. They do not have as much nutritional value as the other foods available for birds.

Pellets

Pellets are available in all pet stores and are a mixture of various ingredients. In theory, it is believed that pellets are able to provide all round nutrition for the bird and are enough as the only meal you give your birds. Of course, you need to supplement the food with a lot of fresh foods.

Like any other commercially available pet food, you will find various brands of pellets. If you are unsure of which one is best for your bird, you can consult an avian vet.

Whenever in doubt, all you need to do is read up about the ingredients mentioned on the packaging. Choose the brand that has minimum preservatives. You must also compare the nutrition content per serving.

Fruits and vegetables
Fresh food is a must for birds to thrive. Fruits and vegetables make up a large portion of Finch food in the wild. Therefore, it is essential that you include it in your regular diet as well.

Remember, fruits and vegetables provide the best source of minerals and vitamins for the birds. These foods are also lower in fats, making them the most suited option for your pet.

In addition to all of this, birds tend to adore the idea of eating fruits and vegetables because of the color of these foods. Each bird will pick his favorite fruit or vegetable. You will be able to understand this by offering all options and seeing which one excites your bird the most.

Make sure you provide your bird with organic produce. That way, you can be sure of minimal pesticide usage. You must also wash the fruits and vegetables thoroughly before giving it to your bird. Some bird owners suggest that you warm the fruits and vegetables slightly in order to make it easy for your bird to digest them.

You can provide almost all fruits and vegetables to your bird. However, you must avoid avocado at all times as it is toxic. It is also a good idea to avoid iceberg lettuce. Although it does not really cause any harm, it is of no nutritional value to your bird.

The best choice of fruits and vegetables include:

- Bell peppers
- Beets
- Apples

- Broccoli
- Butternut squash
- Cilantro
- Collard greens
- Carrots
- Dandelion greens
- Corn on the cob
- Mangoes
- Mustard greens
- Pumpkin
- Papaya
- Peaches
- Sweet potatoes
- Spinach
- Zucchini
- Tomatoes

Whenever possible give your bird fresh foods. Frozen fruit and vegetables may be given occasionally. However, these fruits and veggies do not provide as much nutrition as the fresh produce.

All fruits and vegetables that are large in size must be chopped well or grated before giving the bird any. As for leafy greens, leave them whole as your bird will love to pluck out pieces using his beak. This is a wonderful stimulation activity for your bird

3. Exercise
Gouldian Finches need ample exercise in order to stay healthy. However, you will not have too many chances to get the bird out of the cage. So make sure that the cage is entertaining for the birds. Training is very limited in the case of Finches. You can teach them very basic commands such as "Step up". Here are some ways to make sure your bird gets enough exercise.

Toys
Even in the wild, right from the time when they are born, young birds are given toys to entertain themselves and stay mentally sharp. The cage must have a variety of toys. If you have several toys for your birds, don't just place them all in the cage. Keep a separate toy

box. Keep adding and removing toys. That way, they have something new to look forward to every time.

You may find that it is creatively stimulating to decorate the cage with several toys. But, for the birds, it means restricted space and possible injuries. If you have toys that are hard to clean, keep them away from the area where the birds defecate or feed. Whenever you change the toys in the cage, inspect them to make sure that there is no damage that can be dangerous for the bird. This includes sharp edges, crevices where the beak or feet may get stuck etc.

Suspended toys are extremely entertaining for the birds. But the material that you suspend them with can cause damage. So, make sure that you only use plastic ties or stainless steel links. Using bread ties or gal wires can be very toxic for the birds.

Training
Even with birds like Gouldian Finches, some basic training is required to make them easier to interact with. These birds are trainable to some extent and will respond to training if it is consistent and regular.

When you begin training a Gouldian Finch, it is important to remember that they are not as human oriented as Parrots. So, it may take much longer to train a Gouldian Finch. If you have Parrots or have friends who have any birds from the Parrot family, you need to understand that your progress with your bird will be a lot slower.

Hand raised birds are certainly easier to train. However, all birds can be trained if you get it right in the initial period. When you start training is the most crucial thing. It is best that you start when your bird is fully settled in the new cage.

It takes about a week for your Finches to get used to their new home. These birds are categorized as "high strung" when it comes to training. So, you have to give them a lot of time to settle down.

Begin by getting the bird used to your hand. You need to place your hand in the bird's territory for some time. Offer treats like fruits or seeds when you do so. That way your bird will begin to associate your hand with positive reinforcement.

Repeat this until your bird is comfortable around your hand. There are chances that the bird will voluntarily alight on your finger if you try this consistently.

Finger training Finches
It takes a lot of time to finger train Finches. But considering that these birds live up to 15 years of age or more, it is an important skill to teach your bird to make sure that you are able to get them away from situations that could be dangerous for them.

Try the above mentioned process until the bird recognizes your hands as the source of the treat. The next step is to make sure that the bird comes to your hand and is willing to sit on your finger.

One trick that really helps is holding the treat just behind your finger and waiting for the bird to approach you. When the bird is comfortable enough, he will simply step up on your finger.

Continue this on a daily basis until your bird is sitting on your finger as soon as he sees it. The first step is to finger train your bird inside the cage before you actually let him out.

Getting the bird out of the cage
You need to study the body language of the bird. If he looks comfortable on your finger, you can take him out of the cage for a few minutes.

When you do this, you have to make sure that the area is safe for him. That means the doors and windows need to be shut, the fans need to be turned off and the pets in your household should be away from the area.

Take the Finch out and keep him on your finger for a few minutes outside the cage. In case he decides to fly away, it is a good idea to keep the cage door open and stay close to prevent the other birds from flying out.

After a few minutes, the bird will want to return to his companions. Having a bird who is hand trained is easier to catch if he does not return on his own. That is why it is mandatory to carry out initial training inside the cage before you actually let him out. When he is back in the cage, give him a few treats to know that it is a positive space for him to go back to.

Show training

Showing Gouldian Finches is a very popular hobby amongst the owners. These birds are extremely good looking and can bring you several laurels if you manage to train them for shows and exhibitions.

It is best to train these birds in pairs. They need to first learn about the show cage. It is best that you remove them from their regular enclosure and then set them into the show cage without any distractions such as toys or accessories.

Then, watch the birds. If they are comfortable with one another, you can start training them to step up on your finger or on a perch. There are several other tricks you can teach your bird if you are really patient with them. They will learn to hop over obstacles etc. with the simple target training method.

According to the Gouldian Finch Society, you need to watch out for feather plucking. If that occurs with your birds, it means that they are not compatible and need to be put into separate cages. You can try combinations of different birds to ensure that pairing is suitable and compatible.

4. Hygiene

Keeping your bird clean is one of the most important aspects of care. This ensures that the bird does not have any infections related to parasites or dirt in the cage or on their bodies. Generally, birds love to stay in a clean environment and will get extremely stressed when they are unkempt.

Grooming

The only grooming activity with respect to Gouldian Finches is bathing them. Clipping the wings is strongly advised against. If you provide the bird with toys and perches, they will not require any nail and beak trimming either.

Birds keep themselves clean with these two methods:

- Normally the feathers of the birds will produce some dander or powdery substance. When the down feathers break, the powder is coated on the bird's body. This prevents any dirt from sticking on the body and even makes the feathers water resistant as well.

- All birds use their beaks to preen themselves. They will pick some water up from the bowls and use it to preen. This allows all the feathers to stay in place. In addition to that, preening will break the Uropygial gland that is present just below the tail. Rubbing the oil released from this gland makes the body water resistant. Finches will also preen one another.

Besides the natural cleaning methods, it is a good idea to give your bird a bath once every fortnight. You cannot use soap or scrub the bird clean unless he is hand tamed. In any case, soap is only recommended if you have some very difficult dirt to remove. But, there are four effective methods that will guarantee that your bird takes a bath regularly and will also have a good time while doing so:

Using a bird bath
This is the safest method for small birds like Finches. You can fill the bird bath with warm water. Make sure that the water is just deep enough for the bird to wade around and splash around in. Finches cannot swim and will drown if the water is too deep. Hand tamed birds can be led to a bird bath anywhere in the house. Then, if needed you can use a little soap and gently scrub of any dirt with a washcloth. If you do use soap, rinsing it off fully is a must.

If your bird is not hand tamed, place the bird bath inside the cage. Finches are extremely curious and will walk up to the bird bath and clean themselves. It is a good idea to always have a bird bath in the cage.

Under the tap
This is a method that only works for hand tamed birds. All you have to do is put the tap on so that the water flow is gentle. Avoid showers, as Finches are really small. Then cup your hands such that the tips of your fingers touch the water while your bird sits on the palm. If your bird wants to take a bath, he will walk to the water himself. However, if he shows signs of fear or discomfort, withdraw the bird immediately.

Misting

This is another method that is perfect for birds that have not been tamed. Fill a spray bottle with water and gently mist the wings of the bird from outside the cage. In case your bird is enjoying the mist, he will preen, lift his wings and even lean towards the water spray. However, if he tries to hide and run away, you must stop immediately. This shows that he is not enjoying the spray and is actually asking you to stop. If you continue to spray in this case, you will make your bird dislike baths.

Lettuce tray

This is a fun bath method for the birds. All you need to do is fill up a tray with some water. Then add a few fresh lettuce or spinach leaves into the water. The birds will splash around and play. This is a very stimulating experience as the birds also forage through the leaves and nibble them. Using leaves imitates natural ponds that have plants growing on the surface or inside. Birds in the wild will use these leaves to entertain themselves as they also get clean. It is quite distressing for birds.

What you need to make sure when you give your bird his first bath is to make it a fulfilling experience. If the bird withdraws, don't push too hard. Then, they will have negative associations with bathing and will never let you give them a bath. You can use treats if the bird behaves himself during a bath.

Cage maintenance

The bedding that you choose is an important part of hygiene. You need to make sure that whatever you choose is highly absorbent in nature. Some of the best options for Finch cages include paper towels, computer paper, newspaper, paper bags, butchers' paper or just about anything that absorbs well.

Every night before you turn the lights out, you need to make sure that you take the substrate out and replace all the soiled layers.

The cages and perches should be cleaned out every week with mild liquid dish soap. You can scrub them well to make sure that any dry feces is removed entirely.

Disinfecting the cage once a month is essential. A weak solution of bleach that is about 1 gallon of water with ¾ cup of bleach should do the trick. This will get rid of all the organic substances including feces, food and feathers. You need to remove as much as you can manually before you apply this solution on to the cage.

Remove the birds from the cage when it is being cleaned. It is a good idea to have a small transfer cage that they can be housed in on a temporary basis. Bleach may be used only when the area is well ventilated. You should not use this solution on any metallic surfaces.

The cage should be dried fully before your birds are allowed into the cage. The birds must not come in contact with bleaching powder at any cost. You need to rinse the cage well and dry it in the sun before the birds are replaced.

Physical cleaning of the cage on a regular basis is one of the best ways to prevent diseases amongst your flock. One risk factor for the owners of birds is the inhalation of fecal dust and spores while cleaning the cage. This may aggravate respiratory problems.

The best thing to do would be to install an electrostatic type filter for the air. If your bird area has a central air system, you can prevent the transfer of pathogens.

Of course, all the food and water dishes must be cleaned everyday. If you see any food in the bowls, you need to discard it and make sure that your birds get fresh food every single day. That will keep them healthy and will prevent the chances of any fungal or bacterial growth inside the enclosure.

5. Safety
Your bird's safety is the biggest priority once you bring one home. You need to make sure that your bird is safe even when you are travelling. Unless you take your bird with you, making necessary arrangements to ensure that all care requirements are met is a must.

Bird Proofing
Many bird owners make the mistake of putting the process of bird proofing their home until after they have trained the bird to get out of the cage. This is a big mistake. You can never rule out the possibility of a chance escape when you have the cage door open for

feeding or cleaning. If your house is not bird proofed, then you may have fatal consequences. So, when you decide to bring home pet Finches, the most important thing to do is to make sure that your home is safe for them. This process is almost like baby proofing a home.

The first thing that you need to do is get rid of your polytetrafluoroethylene pans or Teflon pans. You must at least ensure that the kitchen is far away from the enclosure if you want to continue to use them. You see, when these utensils overheat, a certain gas is emitted. This gas is toxic for most birds, especially the Parrot species. Some iron boxes and room heaters also use this material. Make sure that your bird is away from them.

Then, you need to remove any lead items from your home. They are commonly found in wall paint, the curtain weights, some imported artefacts or even the enclosure of the bird itself. Lead is poison for Finches. So, when you are buying a cage, make sure that you test the quality out first. Also, things like the curtain weights become common objects of interest for birds. So, get rid of them.

Smoking indoors is prohibited if you have Finches. They are extremely sensitive to any pollutant in the air. In fact, in the earlier days, people took birds like canaries when they went mining. If there were any pollutants in the air, the birds would react to them immediately. Your Finches may develop pulmonary diseases if you leave them exposed to secondary smoke. If the bird picks any nicotine tar on its body, especially the feet, it becomes so noxious that it actually chews on that part and injures itself.

Toilet seats should always be kept down. There are many instances when birds have drowned in toilets. With tiny birds like the Finch, this is more likely to happen. So, be extremely cautious.

All the wires should be concealed. Usually, they are the favorite toys for your Finches. Tugging and biting electric cords can have serious repercussions. If your birds can fly, they may even get cut or injured by flying straight into these wires.

If there are any plants in the space occupied by the finch, you need to confirm that it is not poisonous for your bird. You may call the National Animal Poison Control Center Hotline on 800-548-2423/

900-680-000. These calls will cost you about $30 per call. They can tell you if a particular plant is poisonous or not. If you unable to confirm this, get the plants away from your bird's immediate environment and wait until you have spoken to an avian vet before you put them back.

In case you have not had your birds' wings clipped, you need to take additional precautions. You need to remove large mirrors to prevent any flight related injuries. Ceiling fans must be removed or kept off unless you know that the bird is in the cage. Windows should be covered with a curtain. Birds that fly into windows or mirrors can injure their necks very badly. Of course, windows should be kept closed at all times to prevent any escape. This is the biggest cause of pet loss.

Lastly, you must be very careful about the stove or any other hot surface like the radiator. You should be able to find covers for these surfaces to ensure that your birds do not get burnt or scalded.

If you have other pets like a cat or a dog, you must keep them in a carrier or keep them chained. Cat saliva is toxic for Finches. Also, if your cat or dog is not properly introduced to the new family member, they will most likely attack them. As for the Finches, they do not stand a chance of survival when attacked by these animals that are natural predators.

When you are away
There could be times when you have to make a temporary trip out of town. That is when you will need someone to care for your Finch in your absence.

The first option is to ask a friend or a relative to pitch in to take care of your bird. If they can stay in your home and do so, it is the best option for the bird. It is less stressful for your birds. Make sure that the person you ask is completely trustworthy.

In case you are unable to find someone who can make time for the bird, the next option is to ask your vet if he has a pet hostel facility where your bird can stay while you are away. He may be able to recommend a reliable option if he doesn't. Make sure that you go and check the facility out if this is the first time the bird is going there.

The last measure that you can take is hiring a pet sitter. There are several professional agencies such as the Pet Sitters International and the National Association of Pet Sitters where you can look for a pet sitter in your area.

The National Association of Professional Pet Sitters lays down some guidelines that will help you find a good sitter for your bird:

- The sitter must have a commercial liability insurance. Then, in case there is some problem with your bird you may hold them responsible for it.

- Ask for recommendations from previous clients. A good sitter will not have any problem connecting you with them.

- Make sure that all the costs involved are on paper. That way neither of you is in the dark about the possible expenditure.

- Meet the person who will be sitting your bird and introduce your bird to them.

- While you are interviewing them, keep an eye on their behavior with the bird. If they are comfortable and easy going with the bird, then it is likely that they have good experience too.

- All the services that the sitter will provide should be mentioned in the agreement. One important clause is with respect to the vet. In case your bird falls sick or has an emergency, the sitter that you hire must be able to deal with it efficiently.

- What will the sitter do if he is unable to show up due to illness or any other emergency? Make sure that he or she has a back up.

Once you are satisfied with all the answers provided by the sitter, you need to make a contract. Ensure that you leave a list of things that he or she may feed the bird, details of any illnesses and the number of your vet.

Chapter 5: When the Bird is home

The biggest challenge begins when you bring your bird home. You need to make sure that the bird is comfortable. The first few days can be extremely challenging as you do not want to stress the bird out. This is when the bird is under a lot of stress considering the travel from the breeder's or pet store to your home.

1. Helping the bird settle in
If you think that the first day consists of endless playing and petting, you are mistaken. It is everything but that.

To make the settling in process easy for the bird, the first step is to set the enclosure or the bird cage up in a quiet and calm enclosure. Here are some tips about setting your bird's new home up:

- Make sure that the cage is placed in a way that the bird is able to see the family and all their activities. However, do not place the cage where it will be in the center of your movements. Placing the cage in a corner or against the wall is a good idea. Don't allow anything like a table obstruct the view of your bird. That way, whenever the members of the family approach him, he will be shocked because he is unable to see them properly.

- Never place the cage near or in the kitchen. The fumes emitted by Teflon coated utensils can be deadly for the bird. The smell of your cooking is also alien to the bird and may make him nervous.

- The enclosure should be in a place that is free from any noise, especially the noise of traffic. There must be enough sunlight during the day and complete darkness at night to let your bird sleep. A bedroom is a great place to house your birds for the first few days.

- If you want to place toys in the cage, make sure that you limit it to just a few in the initial period. The colors can be overwhelming for the bird. So, opt for natural perches and

50

wooden items as toys. The perch must never be over the food bowl or your bird may learn to poop in them and make it a habit.

When you get home, just place the opening of the travelling cage or the box towards the opening of your bird's new enclosure and allow him to walk in. They may take a few minutes or more to do this. Be patient. Once the bird has entered his new enclosure, just close the opening and leave the bird alone. Watch him explore the cage. He will climb, bite, nip at the toys and just approach everything with great caution. This is really fun to watch.

Allow the bird to settle
It will take your bird three days or less to get used to the new home and surroundings. In that time, do not force your love upon the bird. They will treat you like a threat if your stand over the cage and try to talk to them or look at them. Whenever you approach the cage, make sure that you are at the eye level of your bird. This will teach your bird that you are an equal who means no harm.

On the first day, you will not talk to the bird or even go near the cage except to feed him or change the lining of the cage. At this time, the bird will either go away from you or will try to bite and nip. So, wearing gloves is a great idea. Even if your Finch nips or screams, be calm. Pretend like he does not exist and just get on with the cleaning or feeding. When you are done, calmly close the door and walk away.

Around day 3, you can introduce yourself to your bird. Just place your hands on the sides of the cage and sit before the bird at his eye level. Do not move or talk. Just wait till the bird approaches your hand. He will nibble and even lick your hand. The idea is to get the bird used to your smell and presence. With hand bred birds, you can even do this on the second day.

When your bird is a little comfortable, try to stroke the head through the cage. If he backs off or struggles away, then stop immediately. If he is comfortable, however, you can introduce him to your voice. Say hello to your bird in a very gentle tone. Don't talk too much.

Just a few words should be enough just to introduce the bird to your voice.

Try to bring home a few treats for your bird. Your breeder will be able to tell you what treat the bird responds to the best. Treats are a great tool to reduce stress. They will also make the bird approach you voluntarily.

For the next few days, keep the interaction with your bird limited. Just go about your daily business. Whenever you are approaching the cage, say hello to your bird. Finches are a species of Parrots. So, you must expect these birds to be highly intelligent. Even when you are not interacting with them, they have an eye on you. If they see that you are calm in the environment and that you are safe there, they will learn to trust that they are in a place of safety, too.

It is always a good idea to spend the whole of the first day with your bird. You don't have to interact. However, it is good if the bird has an opportunity to watch you all day. So, choose a day when you are likely to be home as the first day of your bird with you and your family.

Note: If you are bringing a baby Finch home, you need to keep millet spray ready for the bird to eat. This is a major part of the diet. In addition to that, if your bird is stressed or scared, he may not eat other foods properly. However, millet spray is something that they should be able to consume easily. For the first two weeks, you can give your baby bird this food.

Educate your family

Before you bring a Finch home, your family must be given a set of guidelines to make sure that they are not adding to the stress of the new member. Here are some things that you should tell your family:

- For the first few days, the cage shall not be approached by anyone else but the designated family member. This could be you, your spouse or parent. Only one person will deal with the feeding and handling for the first few days.

- Nobody will play loud music in the house until the bird gets comfortable enough to feed properly and respond positively to his new environment.

- Existing pets, especially cats and dogs, will not be allowed anywhere near the cage.

- There will not be any visitors for the bird until you are sure that the bird is not afraid of you and your family to begin with.

- Slamming doors shut should be avoided. Any sudden noise is not received well. This also includes blaring the horn in the driveway.

- Talking to the bird should be restricted for at least the first week. New voices are stressful for the bird.

- Do not take pictures with your new Finch. They are not used to the sound of the camera or the flash. This will trigger aggression in your bird.

- Make sure that the environment of the bird does not consist of large or colorful objects. This can trigger a defense instinct in the bird, making them squeak, flap their wings and even nip. If you notice any object in the room that could be a possible trigger, take it out immediately.

- Feeding the bird from your hands should be restricted for the first few weeks. You see, our hands are perceived as a threat by most birds. So, unless you build trust with your Finch, you must not feed with your hands. It is possible that your bird also looks at your fingers as food. They will go straight for it, causing a reaction such as a scream from you. Be warned that this encourages the bird to bite more and learn that habit.

Besides this, your family needs to know that Finches can be extremely noisy. They may also scream endlessly for the first few days. All they are doing is trying to call out to their flock back at the breeder's place or the pet store. Although this can be annoying, you have to learn to deal with it until the bird has been trained well. Besides this, talk to your family in detail about Finches, the type of behavior that these birds will display and the care that they need. The more they learn about the new pet, the better care they will be able to provide.

2. Introducing the bird to other birds

Finches are timid birds, no doubt. However, not all varieties of Finches are compatible with one another. Some of them can get really aggressive when kept in a mixed aviary.

With respect to Finches, a mixed aviary refers to different types of Finches and not different species of birds entirely. The rule of thumb with Finches is that they are best when kept with birds that are of the same physical structure as them. This includes canaries and other Finches. Large birds like Parrots or Cockatoos may not be the best option if you want to house the birds together.

Compatibility among Finches is best understood when you study the nature of the birds in the wild. If they are social birds that are not restricted to pairs, then they will most likely get along well. However, if these birds get too territorial during the breeding season, you may want to study a little more about them before you keep them together.

It is best that you house your birds in pairs if you are going to keep them in a mixed aviary. You must at least ensure that there are equal numbers of male and female birds. That way the competition during the mating season will reduce, leading to less aggression.

If you already have an aviary or even a pet bird at home, the first thing you need to do is quarantine the new bird. You see, birds tend to be carriers of several diseases that can affect the whole flock. Even a seemingly healthy bird may develop health problems after the incubation period of these disease carrying microbes is completed.

The new bird must be kept in a separate cage in an entirely different room for at least 30 days. This is the incubation time of most of the parasites and microbes. If your bird shows any signs of illness within this period, you may return him to the pet store or the breeder if you have a valid health guarantee.

A health guarantee is normally provided for 90 days after the purchase of the bird. However, you need to make sure that the bird is checked by an avian vet within 72 hours of purchase.

The quarantining room should have a separate air source. This means, you can keep the new bird indoors if the other aviary is an outdoor one. It is best that you keep the new bird in a different room altogether. Some even recommend asking a friendly neighbor to keep your new bird for a few days.

Make sure you handle the birds that are already in your home before you handle the new bird. This includes feeding, changing water containers etc. If you do handle the new birds first, take a shower and change your clothes and shoes before you handle the existing birds.

During this time you may want to treat your new bird for parasites such as coccidian, giardia etc. Stoll samples not more than 42 hours old should do the trick.

After quarantining, you can bring the cage of the new bird into the same room as the other birds. If the other birds are larger birds, it is best that you do not house them in the same enclosure. If they are Finches or sparrows, you will have to observe the birds well before you place them together.

Once you keep the cages in the same room, observe the reaction of the other birds. Do they become irritable and aggressive? If yes, you may consider keeping them in separate enclosures. However, if the other birds merely respond to the calls of the new bird, which will make them noisier than usual, it may not be such a bad idea to introduce your birds.

You can introduce the birds by putting them in a neutral enclosure. That way, neither bird is territorial and aggressive. Individual interactions starting with the least aggressive bird is the best option.

Once all the birds in your aviary have been introduced to one another, you can try to place your new Finches in the mixed aviary too. Even the slightest sign of aggression means that you need to get your new bird out and house him separately.

There are a few things that will help you decide if certain birds will be compatible or not. First, you need to understand the habitat of the bird. Birds that are comfortable feeding off the floor of the aviary will usually be less aggressive. On the other hand, if the bird species has special requirements with respect to the feeding area, the nesting spot, etc., they are aggressive.

These birds tend to hijack the nesting areas of other birds leading to a lot of confrontations and aggression amongst one another. If you do have such birds in your aviary which includes the Java Sparrow, Diamond Fire Tail Finch, Cut Throat Finch, Red Brown Finch or the Crimson Finch, it is best that you do not mix your birds.

When you house mixed birds in one cage, you are creating a colony. So, always ask your vet or breeder if a certain species is a colony bird or not. Gouldian Finches, for example, are successful colony birds. But, if you mix them with other species that aren't, you will be putting your birds at risk.

Even with successfully colonized birds, making sure that they get their individual space is mandatory. This means that each bird should have at least 2 cubic meters to himself. They also need to have their own perches and toys and also feeding containers that are easy to access and use. That way, you will have a peaceful colony of birds.

3. Introducing the bird to other pets

If you have a pet cat or dog at home, the choice of letting them interact with your Finch is something that you need to really think about. Yes, there are several instances when these animals bond very well. However, the truth is that the cat or a dog is a natural predator that poses some amount of threat for a Finch.

If you want to introduce your pet cat or dog to the Finch, you need to take a lot of caution. First, you need to let them stay in the same room with the bird inside a secure cage. Then, watch how they react. Naturally, the cat or dog will be inquisitive and will sniff around the cage. Allow that. Make sure you are supervising. If your Finches get agitated or aggressive take your pet away. If you see your pet perching on the cage, this is especially if you have a cat, discourage it.

There will be a point when the pets are so used to each other that they will simply ignore each other. The mistake that most pet owners make is never letting the cat or dog know of the presence of the bird and vice versa. Then, in case of a chance meeting, it may cause a lot of stress to both the pets alike. When you notice that your cat or dog is not reacting to the movements of the Finch including the flutter of wings or the calls of the bird, then you know that they have no interest in the bird. That is when you may bring the bird out of the cage and introduce it to the cat or dog. If you see any aggressive behavior, stop the interaction immediately. If you just say No! sharply to your cat or dog, they will back off. This is only if you have trained them well. If your pet is not trained, this is not a safe option.

Now, some pets are really wonderful souls. They are kind and friendly. They will even have the same approach towards the Finch. However, the sad part is that the size of the animals is so different that even a friendly nip can be fatal for the bird. In case you have a cat, it is advisable to never let them interact without the cage. Cat saliva is known to be fatal for Finches.

It is never a good idea to leave your pets in the same room, unsupervised. You can never control the instinct of an animal fully. If you left the cage door open accidentally, you never know what repercussions that will have. Most likely your Finch will be injured severely or even killed. In some very lucky instances, the animals will bond really well and leave each other unharmed. Now, that is a chance that you cannot take.

In case there is any accident involving your current pet and the Finch, never blame the animal. It is usually the carelessness of the owner that leads to these mishaps. The animals only react as per their first instinct. So, whenever you are leaving your home, make sure that you lock the cage of your Finch securely. You can also keep the dog and cat in separate spaces.

Dogs and cats may or may not bond with your Finch and vice versa. This is a bond that you must never force as it will have untoward consequences.

4. Managing Finch breeding

It is a joy to watch Gouldian Finches breed and take care of their young. During the mating season, the male birds will sing to the females and begin the courting period. This is when he will also choose a suitable mate and perform the mating dance. When this ritual begins, it means that the birds are ready to breed. The male will attempt to mount the female after this dance and if she is willing, they will mate.

Gouldian Finches are prolific breeders in captivity. They will breed quite readily at that. It is necessary that you provide the right conditions for the birds once they are mature and ready to breed.

Usually Gouldian Finches mature really fast. They are ready to mate by the time they are 12 weeks old. However, many breeders recommend breeding them after 6 or 9 months in order to produce healthy offspring.

Preparing for nesting

These preparations should be made when you see that your Finches start displaying courtship behavior, before the actual mating occurs. You might want to have a separate nesting or breeding cage. This should be placed in a quiet and secluded room. Usually a nesting cage is only recommended when you have an aviary or when you are housing more than two birds in a cage. A smaller cage is a good idea to encourage breeding among the birds.

Unlike popular belief, even the nesting cage should have ample entertainment for the bird. Many breeders will tell you that having toys in the cage will distract the birds and prevent mating. However, birds that are happier are most likely to breed. A Finch is only happy when he is entertained.

Nesting box

Once you have decided where you want to place the birds in the breeding season, you need to figure out where they will lay the eggs. This requires a nesting box. You may get separate Finch nesting boxes in stores. Buy one of them and you will find them extremely handy, season after season.

These boxes usually have a door with a raised platform. This is a good idea because there are no chances of damage to the eggs because of the birds rushing into the next box.

That said, the doors need to open and close very easily. If they are tight, it makes it hard for you to open them and inspect the eggs. If the door gets tight for some reason, you can simply sand the edges to make it move easily and freely.

Some people put the nesting box outside the cage. It is recommended that you keep them inside the cage and hang them up on a height. This will reduce any chances of accidents and mishaps. The nesting box should be away from any harsh sunlight.

Nesting material
Depending upon the place that you live, you can figure out the nesting material. The only thing that eggs need to hatch is humidity. So if the place that you live in is very dry you can use wet palm fronds to make the nesting material. This also provides a good foraging surface that your birds will simply love. The birds will take shreds of these fronds into their nesting box and actually build a nest of their own.

There are other things that you may use including shredded paper towels or dry grass. In case the birds are not satisfied with the nesting material provided by you, they will just put their own feathers down.

Keep changing the nesting material even after the eggs have been laid. This will keep the cage fresh. You can source this material from any local pet store. Always check if a certain leaf is poisonous for the bird if you want to go the natural way.

Nutritional requirements
Nutrition plays a very important role in keeping the eggs healthy. Even the birds that are breeding need special nutrition in order to take good care of the eggs. While the genes are the primary factors when it comes to determining the health of your bird, the diet is a catalyst in ensuring that your eggs are of good quality.

Nutrition should consist of mainly fresh produce. You can choose wheatgrass if your bird enjoys it. It is an excellent source of nutrition for breeding birds. It is economical and easily available too.

Fresh produce guarantees a good source of minerals and vitamins. Greens and leaves are the easiest foods to give your bird. In addition to that you have specialized pellets that are meant for breeding birds.

When you are choosing foods for your breeding birds, think of all the foods that represent spring. This includes corn, sprouts, sunflower sprouts etc. This will give them the feeling of being in their natural environment.

You can consult your doctor if you need to provide any supplements for the female. They may ask you to include proteins and calcium in a larger amount to aid the formation of healthy eggs.

Artificially incubating the eggs
It is best that you allow the parents to hatch the eggs and then take over the responsibility of feeding the birds by hand in order to make them acquainted with people.

Artificial incubation is not always necessary. There are a few breeding problems that arise making it necessary for you to hatch the eggs in an incubator.

Egg breaking or eating
This is a common issue with birds that have been brought into captivity from the wild. This is only a result of the bird's defensive behavior towards anyone who approaches the nest.

The bird sits or jumps on the egg as an attempt to safeguard it and ends up breaking the eggs. This is when you have to take the following precautions:
- Increase the size of the cage or enclosure.
- Make the nesting box narrower and darker.
- Minimize any activity in the breeding area of the birds and make it as quiet as possible.

In some cases, this habit is repeated with every clutch and is actually just a learnt behavioral pattern. This is when you will have to intervene and incubate the eggs artificially.

Abandonment of the eggs
Smaller birds like Gouldian Finches are notorious for abandoning their eggs. You will face this problem more often with hand raised parent birds who do not have any parenting instinct. This is when you can take one of the following measures:

- Pair a hand raised bird with one raised by the natural parents. That way one is experienced and the other can learn.
- If your hen is not a good breeder, you need to take the decision of taking the bird out of the breeding program. While this may be hard for you to do, you need to understand that these birds are just not meant to care for a clutch.
- If your birds have been good parents in the past, then you need to check the nesting conditions that you have provided. If anything seems out of the ordinary or inappropriate, making necessary changes will prevent abandonment.

If you notice any of the above problems with the clutch, you will have to incubate the eggs artificially. Collect the eggs carefully and place them in a commercially available incubator. You will have the details of all the settings for Gouldian Finch eggs. Once you have set the incubator as needed, you have to follow these measures to make sure that you get maximum hatchability with your eggs:

- Place the incubator in an area that is free from any direct sunlight or drafts.

- The incubator should be sterilized before you place the eggs inside. The web bulb wick and the humidifier must be functioning properly.
- Make sure you wash your hands and clean the eggs thoroughly before you put them in the incubator. They should be free from any dirt or grime.
- The small end or the pointed end of the egg should always be lower than the large end of the egg
- The egg must be turned at least 5 times each day. If you fail to turn the eggs every day, chances are that the chicks that are

developing will get stuck to one side and may be born with the organ sticking out of the body.

- Once you have set the eggs inside the incubator do not disturb them except for when you turn them. While doing so, if you notice that the eggs are still cold, chances are that you have not started the incubator or that it is not functioning properly.
- It is possible to check the progress of your eggs with a bucket of water. In the beginning the eggs will sink to the bottom while towards the end of the incubation period, they will begin to float on the surface.

Once the eggs have hatched, you need to shift the chicks to a brooder. You may choose to place the bird in a commercially available brooder or may make one using a box and the appropriate full spectrum light. The temperature should be around 92 degree F when the birds just hatch. By the 5th day you can reduce this to 80 degree F.

You will have to place absorbent bedding such as newspaper. Keeping the brooder moisture level above 50% is very important. If you are making a brooder at home, you can use a spray bottle to mist the brooder with lukewarm, distilled water. Make sure you only spray around the brooder and never directly at the chick.

Hand feeding your Finches

- You can get the feeding formula from any local pet store. Make a mixture of this formula with hot water and place it in a sterilized container. The formula should be made freshly before every feeding session and should never be stored in the refrigerator.
- Force feeding chicks is strictly prohibited. If you hold up a teaspoon or a syringe to the bird, he should approach you voluntarily. This reduces chances of choking on the food.
- As the chick feeds he will bob his head up and down. You will have to match the rhythm of dispensing food with this rhythm.

- Pause and give the food in short intervals to help the bird swallow better.
- The formula must never fall on the nostrils of the bird. If you notice any on the beak or nostril, clean it immediately.

- Never overfeed the chick. If he stops eating do not force him.
- The crop should empty before you give the bird his feed.

Increase the consistency of the formula with each day. By day 5 you can start weaning the chicks. Leave the food around and see if they eat on their own. By the 8th day, you can stop feeding the bird at night. That will make them hungry enough to eat by themselves. By the time they are 21 days old, they should be fully weaned.

Hand feeding is a great option if you wish to sell the chicks. Most people prefer birds that are already used to human interaction in order to make it easier during the housebreaking phase. These birds are also much easier to train.

In some cases where the parents are caring for their young, you can try mixed feeding. Allow the parent birds to give the chicks one meal and you can give them the next until they are weaned. These are the most sought after types of birds as they have the experience of being parented and are also comfortable around human beings.

Chapter 6: Health of Gouldian Finches

It is a popular belief, as mentioned above, that Gouldian Finches are fragile birds. However, this is not entirely true. When given the right living conditions, these birds can live up to 8-10 years.

In order to keep your bird healthy, it is necessary to understand the health issues that they are most susceptible to. Taking preventive measures or identifying the symptoms of these conditions is crucial to the longevity of your pet bird.

1. Identifying a sick bird

There are several symptoms that help you identify a sick bird. These symptoms can either be mild or intense. In any case, you have to be alert and identify the slightest change or deviation from normal. That can work wonders in saving your bird's life.

Here are a few symptoms that can help you identify illnesses in your birds and provide timely assistance:

- **Fluffed feathers**
  If your bird looks fluffy or puffed up in appearance, it is the most obvious sign of an ill bird. The common reason for fluffing up feathers is to keep him warm.

  When your bird tries to do this, you will see that the regular sleek frame is lost. The bird will actually look fat and extremely messy. Sometimes, birds may just puff up their feathers for some time while preening. But if the puffiness is prolonged, it is a matter of great concern.

  However, puffiness must never be ignored even if the bird retracts the feathers when you approach him. This is a common defense mechanism as the bird does not look vulnerable. You must also be observant of the bird's body language. If the bird looks sick or you have the slightest suspicion, you need to make sure that you pay attention.

- **Wet vent**
  If the vent area of the bird is constantly wet, then it can be considered a symptom of illness. This is the underside of the bird where the bird excretes from. If the bird is healthy, the vent is dry and clean.

- **Respiratory issues**
  One of the most common tells tale signs of sickness in a bird is abnormal or heavy breathing. This type of breathing without any physical exertion means that the bird may be unwell. In addition to heavy breathing the bird will also exhibit tail bobbing.

  If the bird is sneezing, coughing or has some sort of nasal discharge, it is an indication of illness. Hold the bird close to you if you have any suspicion. You may be able to hear a distinct clicking sound which indicates chances of mites or parasites in the air sac. This needs to be checked immediately to help the bird recover at the earliest.

- **Inactivity**
  Finches are usually quite active and love to fly about or just interact with one another. If your bird is sleepy all the time and is found catching untimely naps, it is a warning sign.

  Birds will nap in the afternoons or during the day. However, they seldom nap when the rest of their cage mates are active. If your bird is snoozing while the others are active, you need to look at it as a warning sign.

  Birds that sit at the bottom of the cage for long hours may also be unwell. This is not a common thing especially in an aviary as Finches prefer to interact with one another and will seldom be isolated in this manner. If they have the habit of sitting on the floor of the cage, it will usually be with their partners.

However, if you see that your Finches are shunning the company of other birds, especially their own partners, you need to understand that there is definitely some problem with the bird.

- **Loss of appetite**
  If a bird loses interest in food because of any illness, it is a sign of great concern. Always be observant of your birds. The thing with Finches is that they do not want to appear unwell or sick. They may just pretend to eat the food you have given to them to make sure that they do not look vulnerable. However, they could only be sifting through the food and may not be actually consuming anything.

- **Lack of singing**
  Vocalization is the most important sign of health, especially in Finches. These birds are known for their unique songs and vocalization patterns.

  When birds are unwell they remain unusually silent. The idea behind this is to make sure that they do not attract any unwanted attention from predators.

  In addition to this, birds that are unwell will also do this as a method of saving up on their energy. If a bird who normally loves to chirp and sing becomes abnormally silent, you must immediately take him to your vet.

- **Unusual droppings**
  Whenever you are cleaning out the substrate of the cage, make sure that you check the droppings of the birds. If the droppings are abnormal or have some unusual color, it could be a sign of indigestion or some disease.

  If you have several birds in your aviary that belong to different families and species, this can be a little challenging. However, you can watch out for a few basic things such as the urates which should be white and dry in color. On the other hand if it dries up to look green or yellow, you need to show some concern immediately.

Maintenance of Gouldian Finches depends mostly on simple observation. In case you are unable to spend time watching your birds, you will never become familiar with the regular and normal behavior. As a result, you will also be unable to identify anything out of the ordinary.

In fact, you may miss out on initial symptoms of diseases that can be managed fairly easily. Even if you stop paying attention for a short time, you can miss out on some important behavioral changes that can be pivotal in saving the bird's life.

One thing all bird owners should know about is that birds prefer to hide their illness in order to look fit. In most cases, by the time the symptom becomes obvious, the bird is already very sick.

If you have an aviary, a sick bird is not only a matter of concern because of his health. He is a ticking time bomb that can affect the rest of the flock in no time.

If you are observant and find the symptoms early, you can have the bird quarantined and ensure that the rest of your flock is safe too. You have to first identify that your bird is sick. The next step is to narrow in on which disease it actually is. Lastly, you need to take all the preventive measures necessary for your aviary in order to keep the birds healthy.

2. Common illnesses in Finches

Like all species of birds, the Gouldian Finch is also susceptible to attack and infection by certain microbes. These birds are genetically predisposed to certain conditions and you need to make sure that you take care accordingly.

There are other factors like nutrition and hygiene that also affect the health of your bird to a large extent.

Nutritional diseases

As discussed before, the metabolism in Finches is very high. As a result, their body also demands a lot of nutrients. Birds are quicker than any other creature in the animal kingdom to depict the signs of malnutrition as well.

In many cases, pet birds have been diagnosed with nutritional diseases more often. In most cases, the immunity of the bird towards disease causing organisms is compromised when his nutritional requirements are not met.

It is very common to see birds showcase nutritional problems when they are in the breeding cycle. Problems like calcium deficiency are most prevalent in these birds. This leads to a lot of complications like egg binding or prolapse of the oviduct.

Each species has a different type of response to deficits in nutrition. In case of the finches, you will see a lot of tell gate signs. The most common nutritional diseases in finches include:

Obesity
This is the most common nutritional disorder, often ending in hepatic lipidosis or fatty liver. This condition has been observed in birds that are usually on a high fat seed only diet. This type of diet also leads to other issues like lowered calcium in the blood. Seeds also lack nutrients like vitamin A.

Two organs of the bird's body that are normally affected by obesity are the liver and the heart. Over time, all the fat that has been accumulated in the blood is passed on into the liver. This leads to a drastic decrease in the amount of functional tissue in the liver.

This condition also makes the liver very enlarged. If the fat accumulation occurs around the heart of the bird, the normal functioning of the heart is also compromised.

If the bird is overweight, he is not able to perform simple tasks such as flying or bathing in the water trough.

Symptoms of hepatic lipidosis

- The fat deposits are seen on the abdomen and chest, making these areas look large and buxom.

- The beak tends to grow rather abnormally. This condition is often identified by those who groom the bird and trim the beak at the vet's office.

- You will see obvious black spots on the toenails and the beak. This is primarily because the functionality of the liver is compromised. The clotting of blood does not occur properly leading to bruise like splotches on the beak and the nails.

- The liver is enlarged. Of course, this is not seen visually. When the bird is being checked by the vet, this becomes obvious. In smaller birds like Finches, you can see this enlarged liver through the screen if you just moisten the skin with some alcohol.

These clinical signs are noticed in birds of all species. If you do not curb the fat intake of your bird, the regular bodily functions are largely compromised. Even simple stress like a loud noise can be too stressful for the bird leading to death.

Diagnosis

- Physical examinations are the first step to diagnosis.

- Your vet may also require the blood to be tested for anemia, lipemia or chances of jaundiced plasma which indicate compromised functioning of the liver.

Treatment

The best way to manage this condition is by improving the nutrition of your bird. You can prevent this condition entirely if you are careful about what you are feeding the bird.

Make sure that your bird gets a good balance of homemade food as well as commercially available food for the best possible results.

Some medicines such as probenecid or colchicine can be administered to help birds who have been severely affected.

Hypovitaminosis A
This is yet another condition that you will see in birds that have been maintained on an all seed diet. Most seeds and nuts do not have any traces of vitamin A.

The mucous membrane and the epithelial tissue is maintained by Vitamin A. When the levels of this nutrient drop, resistance to pathogenic or disease causing organisms also decreases.

You will commonly notice infections of the sinus and the respiratory tract in birds that have a deficiency of Vitamin A. You will also notice scaliness, flakiness and thickening of the skin of the bird's feet.

Symptoms of Vitamin A deficiency

- White plaques are seen on the roof of the mouth.

- A change in the functionality of the tear glands and the salivary glands leads to high levels of oral mucous.

- Respiratory difficulty accompanied by problems like coughing are quite common in birds with this condition.

- When the lack of vitamin A leads to compromised immunity, it manifests in the form of abscesses in the respiratory tract, the crop and the oral cavity of the bird.

- In case of brightly colored birds such as Gouldian Finches, the coloration of the plumage will also fade away with time.

- The hatchability rate of the clutches will decrease quite drastically.

- The chicks that do hatch may not survive or may fail to gain wait and die eventually.

Treatment

Preventive measures such as a healthy diet and proper supplementation are the best options for your bird. In case your bird develops this condition despite all the care, here are a few things that you can try:

- Provide commercial feed that is fortified with Vitamin A. These foods are often given along with water.

- The amount of orange and red vegetables as well as green leafy vegetables should be increased in your bird's diet.

- You can provide your bird with beta-carotene supplements. In most clinical cases this supplement is injected.

- Add a few drops of the extracts from a Vitamin A gel capsule into your bird's food.

- Cod liver oil can be added to your bird's diet. This is also quite easy to mix with dry foods like pellets and seeds.

With a balanced vitamin A intake, you will notice that your birds become more and more resistant to common health issues. You will also notice a very positive change in the reproductive cycle and results with regular Vitamin A supplements.

Hypervitaminosis A
Just as the deficiency of nutrients can lead to a lot of health problems, an excess of the same nutrient can be toxic to the bird. Many bird owners tend to over-supplement the diet of their birds leading to several complications.

The only sad thing is that this is a poorly documented condition among birds. In the case of other animals, it has been seen that an excess of vitamin A in the body leads to a lot of fatigue and weakness in the bird. It can also lead to pain in the bones.

Calcium, Vitamin D3 and Phosphorous imbalance
If the diet of your bird consists mainly of oily seeds and grains, you will notice these imbalances. These foods have a very low ratio of phosphorous to calcium and are also deficient in Vitamin D3. Additionally, the calcium that is available to the bird is bound within the body in the form of soaps when the diet is too oily.

Calcium is one of the most important minerals as far as the birds are concerned. The production of the egg is highly hampered when the calcium intake is not good enough. Calcium is also required by the skeleton of the bird. If calcium and phosphorous are not absorbed properly, it can lead to bones that are underdeveloped or extremely fragile.

There are several other body functions such as the transmission of nerve impulses, muscle contractions and also metabolic processes that are affected by the calcium levels in the body.

Calcium metabolism is affected by the amount of Vitamin D3 and phosphorous in the bird's body. Therefore, providing only calcium is meaningless as it will not be utilized properly.

Ideally, the ration of calcium to phosphorous should be 2:1 in the body of birds like Finches. This value can have a 0.5 variation and not more.

Symptoms of calcium, vitamin D3 and phosphorous imbalance

- Adult birds are highly uncoordinated in muscle function when there is an imbalance.

- Weakness is commonly seen in birds with this nutritional deficiency.

- Egg binding as well as paresis or fatigue is seen in egg laying birds that do not have enough calcium available in their diet.

- In the case of chicks you will see that deformities in the bone and joint are very common.

- Spay leg formation is seen in birds that have less calcium intake.

Treatment

Supplementation is the best option when your bird has calcium deficiency. However, you need to be very careful when you are giving these supplements to your birds.

If not done properly, excessive amounts of phosphorous and calcium can lead to other complications.

If the level of calcium is beyond the necessary amount, it can lead to mineralization of the kidney and kidney failure. When calcium is available in large amounts, the absorption of essential trace elements like zinc and manganese is affected.

If the level of phosphorous is too high, it is seen that calcium is not absorbed properly. This is because any calcium in the body will be bound in the form of calcium phosphate that is not soluble. As a result, blood calcium level will be low.

You need to make sure that you do not provide any unwanted supplements if the natural foods are able to provide your bird with all the nutrients that he requires.

Imbalance in Vitamin D
The main function of Vitamin D is to make sure that calcium metabolism occurs in the body of the bird. Vitamin D can be equally problematic if the levels are either too low or too high.

If the diet of the bird consists of an excessive amount of Vitamin D, it leads to toxicosis which means that the amount of calcium absorbed by the body also increases drastically. In the initials stages, this is not an issue as the kidney is able to excrete the excess calcium out.

But with repetitive calcium excess, the function of the kidney is compromised leading to a reduced rate of glomerular filtration. As a result, kidney stones are formed and can be extremely painful for your birds.

There are several factors such as the form of Vitamin D ingested, the amount of calcium and vitamin A in the diet etc. that determine the chances of toxicosis. The health of the kidney us another major factor.

For example, providing cholecalciferol vitamin D supplements are more toxic than supplements like ergocalciferol. In fact, the former puts the bird at 10 times more risk than the latter.

If your bird is being over-supplemented with vitamin D, there are chances that the kidney gets mineralized along with calcification of the blood. If you have fed your bird toxic amounts of Vitamin D3, you may balance it out by reducing calcium in the diet.

In case your bird has any nutritional imbalance, the best thing to do would be to provide the bird with a diet that is nutritionally adequate. Getting them on homemade food is the best option. Of course, you also have the option of providing them with recommended commercial foods.

Mineral sources like calcium carbonate that can be found in egg or oyster shells are ideal for Finches. You can also give your bird natural sources like milk, yoghurt, cheese, spinach and broccoli. If you are giving your bird eggs, make sure that it is not raw to reduce any risk of salmonellosis.

Deficiency of iodine
A seed based diet is usually responsible for iodine deficiency in the body. Thyroxine, which is responsible for thyroid gland function, is not formed in the body without adequate amounts of iodine.

It is necessary to give your bird iodine supplements if you are keeping them on a seed only diet. This supplement can be added into the food or water of the bird.

Goiter is the result of iodine deficiency. The thyroid gland is present in the area where the trachea branches out into the lungs. This is just above the heart. As a result, when these glands become enlarged, a lot of pressure is applied on the voice box and the trachea. You will notice that birds have great difficulty breathing when they suffer from iodine deficiency for this very reason.

You will notice a wheeze, click or a squeaking sound whenever your bird tries to breathe. You will also notice vomiting in birds that have an iodine deficiency.

Goiter develops very slowly but gets very bad progressively. The larger the thyroid gets, the more obvious the sounds while breathing become. In many cases, the bird needs to exert himself physically and hold his head up in order to breathe.

There is always a chance of secondary bacterial invasion or fungal infection. This condition also leads to weight gain, deposits of fat on the internal organs, compromised feather quality and a lot of other secondary issues.

Although this is a rare deficiency in Finches, you need to be watchful. The treatment of the condition is determined by the severity of deficiency.

Treatment of iodine deficiency

- In case of a mild deficiency, adding iodine supplements in the food or water can help.

- In extreme cases, your bird may have to be hospitalized to receive sodium iodide injections daily until this condition is reversed.

- Preventive measures are important following the treatment in the form of good diet and necessary supplements.

Hemochromatosis
Iron storage disease or hemochromatosis is very common in Finches and is the result of the bird's inability to excrete any excessive iron. This leads to damage in the heart, kidneys and the liver. Blood breakdown and chronic stress can be caused by hemochromatosis.

Several enzymes are not formed when there is an excess of iron in the body. In addition to that it also leads to genetic predisposition of the hatchlings to this condition.

You will notice difficulty in breathing along with a distension of the abdomen. Discolored droppings are common with birds who have hemochromatosis.

Treatment of hemochromatosis

- Long-term phlebotomies or blood-letting are carried out on a weekly basis in order to reduce the iron deposits.

- The iron levels in blood serum are constantly monitored to ensure that they do not exceed 150mg.

- A hematocrit or CBC is used to make sure that the bird recovers from these blood-letting sessions.

- A medicine called deferozamine has been used to treat this condition as well.

Dietary management is the best way to prevent this condition in your Gouldian Finches. Better diets are available for Finches these days. All you need to do is consult your vet. Bottled water is recommended if your bird has had this condition in the past.

Birds that have not had hemochromatosis and have lived long lives have been given a lot of fresh foods and low amounts of seeds. It is best that you also rely on a balanced diet for your birds to prevent the above mentioned nutritional deficiency.

If you are new to the world of Finches it is recommended that you follow a diet provided by your vet. As you gain more experience with your birds and do your own research, you can mix up the diet. In any case, remember that supplementation without consultation is always prohibited for your birds if you want to ensure that they stay in the best of their health for the rest of their lives.

Bacterial diseases

It is very common for birds to develop bacterial diseases. Most often inappropriate husbandry is responsible for making the birds develop this condition. Improper nutrition leads to compromised immunity that makes the birds more susceptible to these infections.

Juvenile birds and neonates are even more susceptible to these conditions. The respiratory tract and the gastrointestinal tract are the first ones to get affected by these bacteria.

There are various strains of bacteria that affect birds out of which strep, staph, citobacter and E.coli are the most common ones. These are the bacteria that are associated with humid areas, dust, old food, seed, grit and water. In some birds natural resistance to these bacteria may be compromised due to reproductive diseases in the parent.

Most common symptoms of bacterial infection

- Droppings that are watery and green in color.
- Sneezing
- Rubbing the eyes incessantly
- Swallowing constantly
- Coughing
- Yawning
- Coughing
- Change in voice or loss of voice

Bacterial infections, caused by either ingestion or inhalation is life threatening if left unattended. The exact type of bacteria needs to be identified before giving the bird any form of treatment. That it is when you can treat it perfectly and also prevent it from recurring.

Treatment and precautions for common bacterial diseases

- Antibiotics are administered after the culture test is complete.

- Antibiotic drops are given directly to the bird if he is very ill. You can even inject the antibiotics in these cases.

- If the infection is mild, you can administer the antibiotics through drinking water. You need to make sure that the bird is drinking water when you take this approach.

- All the seed, fruit and grit should be removed from the cage.

- Disinfecting the cage on a regular basis is a must.
- The seeds that you provide must be sterile.

- The bird must never be left out of the cage unsupervised.

- If your bird has not recovered fully, you need to make sure that you do not allow him to wander around the house.

There are several things that you can do in order to accelerate recovery in your bird. You can give the birds Turbo-boosters and also energy supplements.

Special Fvite with sterile seeds can be included as a part of the diet of your bird.

Once your antibiotic treatment is complete, you can give your bird loford and dufoplus in water. You need to make sure that your bird is eating and drinking well. If he is not doing so, your vet may have to force feed him.

Bacterial infections can become very severe in the long run. They will damage the kidney and liver if ignored and the bird becomes susceptible to a lot of illnesses in the future.

It is the responsibility of the owner to understand how a certain disease originated in order to help the bird recover faster. In order to ensure that your bird does not have repetitive episodes of infection you can get a complete health program from your vet and follow it till your bird is fully recovered.

Paying attention to bacterial infections is very important as humans can also be affected by certain strains of bacteria. The droppings of the bird can spread bacteria. Children are especially susceptible to infection and must be kept away from a sick bird. One example of a bacterial strain that affects finches and humans is campylobacter.

Remember that bacterial infections are usually related to the surroundings of the bird. If there is any contamination that enters the mouth of the bird, it will lead to the disorder.

Of course, even the best kept birds may be susceptible to infections. If this happens, it becomes even more important for you to make sure that you understand the source of the infection and try your best to prevent any more in the future.

Here are a few strains of bacteria and the common sources of infection for each one of them.

E.coli
- Fluctuation of temperature
- Draught
- Stress
- Contaminated food or old fruit
- Wet areas
- Dirty cages

Strep
- Underlying viral infection
- Cold stress
- Dust
- Poor quality of food
- Stress

Staph
- Mice
- Dust
- Poor seed quality
- Contamination in the air conditioning

Diplococcus
- Stress

- Mice

Citobacter and Pseudomonas
- Poor water conditions
- Poor cage hygiene

Many owners believe in a holistic approach to prevent these infections. You may also try the following after consultation with your vet.

- **Goldensea:** This herb is used for its strong antibiotic property. It is effective against E.coli, staph and strep.

- **Echinacea:** This herb is known for killing several pathogens that cause diseases including protozoa, fungi and bacteria.

- **Licorice root:** This herb is antiviral and antibacterial in nature and is known to be effective against the most powerful strain of bacteria.

Most common bacterial conditions in Finches

In the case of Finches, there are two conditions that you need to be extra cautious about. These birds are genetically predisposed to these conditions and may even be carriers of the condition in some cases.

Chlamydiosis
This is a condition that affects almost all companion birds. It is best that you follow all the federal regulations with respect to testing and quarantining for this condition if you plan to have an aviary or if you plan to breed Finches.

This condition is caused by a type of bacteria called *chlamydia psittaci*. The incubation period of this strain ranges from 3 days to a couple of weeks.

The only concern with this condition is that it is easily transmitted from one bird to another through the feces. They bacteria stays infectious in debris that is organic for more than one month.

Symptoms in birds that are carriers:

- Anorexia
- Nasal and ocular discharge
- Dehydration
- Excessive droppings
- Lack of appetite
- Diarrhea

Symptoms in birds that are clinically ill

- All of the above
- Monoystosis
- Leukocystosis
- Increase in bile acid level

Diagnosis

Diagnosis of this condition is quite difficult as the clinical signs are usually mild or absent. The most common methods of diagnosis include:
- Antigen and antibody tests
- Serological tests
- PCR testing
- Cloacal swab analysis

Multiple diagnosis methods must be applied because of the nature of this condition which is actually quite hard to identify and understand.

Treatments

- Doxycycline is the most common treatment option.
- Dietary calcium must be reduced during this treatment phase.
- Medicated feed may be administered if the condition is too severe.

You need to make sure that you devise a proper treatment plan for this condition as it can be transmitted to people quite easily.

Avian mycobacterosis
This condition is usually caused by different types of bacteria including *Mycobacterium avium, M.intercellulare, M.bovis, M.genovense and M.tuberculosis.*

This condition is progressive and usually affects the gastrointestinal tract of the bird as well as the liver. This condition is hard to diagnose because of the limited number of clinical signs available in the initial stages of infection.

Symptoms of Avian mycobacteriosis

- Weight loss
- Anorexia
- Diarrhea
- Depression

Diagnosis of the condition

- Acid fast staining of the culture
- Biopsy of the intestines, liver and spleen
- PCR testing
- Ultrasound

The difficult part in diagnosis is the fact that these strains of bacteria are very hard to culture. Therefore if the culture test is negative it is not conclusive that the condition does not exist.

The other tests are not as sensitive. The best option is PCR testing of a sample of the bird's feces. In some cases radiographs have been useful in determining the condition.

If you have an aviary with multiple birds, it is also hard to determine which of the birds is actually infected. If you are able to point out the birds that have the highest risk of being affected, you need to make sure that they are isolated and properly monitored.

Treatment

- Antibiotic treatment for 1 year or more
- Administration of multiple antibiotics
- Examination of your own husbandry practices

If your bird is in the advanced stage of this condition, it is less likely that he or she will be able survive. Although there have been no records of the conditions being passed on from birds to humans, you need to make sure that you take all the necessary precautions especially if you have an immunity that is weak.

Viral diseases
Viral infections in birds can be fatal in most conditions. Makings sure that your birds are checked by a vet on a regular basis is the key to keeping birds away from these diseases. With most viral diseases, the incubation period is very short and the birds may succumb to the infection overnight.

Here are some of the avian viral diseases that may affect Gouldian Finches:

Avian polyomavirus
This condition usually affects birds that are young. Usually adult birds are immune and in case of any infection, will shed the virus in just 90 days. Incubation period for avian polyomavirus is 10 days.

Symptoms of avian polyomavirus infection

In the most typical cases, a healthy juvenile bird that is still not a fledgling will develop crop stasis, lethargy and will die in just 48 hours of the onset of the condition. In rare cases, the following symptoms are recorded:

- Abdominal distention
- Cutaneous hemorrhage
- Feather abnormality

Diagnosis of the condition

- Examination of the cloacal swab

- Blood tests
- Virus neutralizing tests
- Antibody tests
- Necropsy testing of the chicks that have succumbed to the condition.

Prevention of the condition

- Keeping the aviary free from visitors.
- Making sure that new birds are only included in the aviary after 90 days of strict quarantining.
- Making sure that you keep up all the practices of hygiene.
- Stopping breeding for at least six months if the condition is diagnosed in any bird in the aviary.
- Disinfection of the nesting boxes and the aviary.
- Avoid purchasing birds from different sources.
- Avoid purchasing birds that have still not been weaned.

Treatment of the condition

As discussed before avian polyomavirus has a very short incubation period
and the symptoms are rarely seen before the bird succumbs to the infection.

You can opt for a vaccine that is available for younger birds. Making sure that you give birds that are breeding a dose of these vaccines at intervals of two weeks in the off-season in a must.

You must also provide these vaccines to neonates before they are 35 days old. You have the option of a booster shot after about 3 weeks as well. Getting your birds this shot prevents the risk of infection to a large extent.

In general, there is no cure for this condition except preventive measures and supportive care after the condition has been diagnosed.

Gouldian Finch Herpesvirus

This is a rather uncharacterized strain of virus that is known to affect Gouldian Finches, Crimson Finches and Red Faced Waxbills. If you have an aviary with multiple birds, you will observe lesions in birds that are affected. However, some of them may be completely unaffected by the virus.

Symptoms of Finch Herpesvirus

- Listlessness
- Ruffled plumes
- Heavy breathing
- Nasal discharge
- Swelling in the eyelids
- Crusts in the cleft of the eyelid
- Inability to eat

After about 5-10 days of the first signs and symptoms of this viral infection, it has been observed that birds are unable to survive. Post necropsy, it was observed that the birds showed thickening of the fibnoid and discharge in the eyes and nostrils. Besides that the internal organs seemed normal on all occasions.

Herpes virus are considered an alpha strain of virus because of which the incubation period is very short and the damage caused is quite serious. There is no cure for these conditions. All you can do is take preventive measures to make sure that the birds are quarantined properly, given ample food and clean water and are kept in the most hygienic conditions possible.

Avian bornavirus

Infections by avian bornavirus in birds were observed quite recently in birds with the first ever records being made in the 1970s. Since then, several species have been considered susceptible to the condition including finches. The first evidence of this condition affecting finches was observed in Estrildid Finches.

This condition is progressive in a few cases or may develop overnight in others. Mortality rates are high in birds that have been affected by this strain of virus.

After several crop biopsies, it was discovered that affected birds have lesions in the heart, the gastrointestinal tract, the brain, spinal cord, lungs and kidneys. The disease may either be transmitted orally or through the feces. It is highly contagious and can be even more problematic if you have a mixed aviary.

Symptoms of avian bornavirus infections

- Chronic weight loss
- Increase in appetite followed by excretion of undigested food
- Regurgitation
- Convulsions
- Weakness
- Tremors
- Ataxia or inability to control movements
- Blindness

Diagnosis

- Biopsy of cloacal swabs
- PCR testing

These tests need to be carried out once every week for three straight weeks to determine if the bird is really infected or not. The virus is shed intermittently which makes it even more necessary for you to have multiple tests as well as differential diagnosis for conditions like toxicosis and foreign body obstruction before the conclusions are derived for infection by the avian bornavirus.

Treatment

- Providing the bird with food that is easy to digest
- Administering medications like celecoxib and meloxicam
- Isolation of infected birds as a method of disease prevention
- Regular PCR tests
- Good hygiene
- Ultraviolet light setting

Poxvirus infection

This is a large DNA virus that usually affects the respiratory tract, the oral cavity and the epithelial cells of the internal organs. It is believed that all birds are susceptible to this condition. In case of aviary birds or companion birds, this condition can be avoided as the birds will not be exposed to this virus if proper husbandry practices are followed.

This disease usually affects Parrots and Finches. In the case of Gouldian Finches, your bird may only be a carrier and may never develop symptoms. However, for those with a mixed aviary, this is also cause for great concern as the disease spreads rapidly.

The infection may be cutaneous or systemic depending upon the strain of virus that has affected your bird, the age of your bird, the health of the bird and the route of exposure.

In the cutaneous form, you will notice that there are wart like growths on parts of the body that are unfeathered including the area around the eyes and nares, the legs and the beak. Another form which is the diptheric form shows similar formations on the larynx, pharynx, tongue and the mucosa. The systemic form is differentiated by the characteristic ruffled appearance of the bird.

Symptoms of poxvirus infection

- Lesions on the eye, ear and oral cavity
- Lethargy
- Troubled or labored breathing
- Difficulty in swallowing
- Partial blindness
- Weight loss
- Skin lesions
- Ruffled appearance

Treatment of poxvirus infection

- Supportive care

- Fluids included in the diet
- Vitamin A supplementation
- Cleaning of the lesions on a daily basis
- Antibiotics
- Ointments for secondary infections
- Assisted feeding
- Mosquito control
- Indoor housing

It is also possible to provide your Gouldian Finches with certain vaccinations that will make them immune to certain strains of pox virus.

Avian influenza
Commonly known as bird flu, this is a condition that affects almost all species of birds. Most of the causal strains of virus do not affect human beings. However, it was recently discovered that some strains like the A(H7N9) cause serious infections in humans as well.

This is a condition that commonly affects waterfowl but can even lead to outbreaks on a large scale in an aviary set up. The virus is so potent that it has the ability to even affect other mammals. So if you have other pets at home, you have to be very careful and watchful.

This disease has a very aggressive progression. This means that the disease can spread within a few hours and can lead to death as well.

Symptoms of avian influenza

- High fever
- Diarrhea
- Vomiting
- Coughing
- Abdominal distension
- Decreased egg production
- Inflammation of the trachea
- Congestion
- Hemorrhage

- Edema
- Lack of limb coordination
- Paralysis
- Blood in the nasal and oral discharge
- Greenish color of the droppings

Treatment

- Vaccination is the best option to prevent the disease altogether

This condition can be serious if the strain of virus that affects the bird can affect humans as well. In many states it is a mandate to report the outbreak of avian influenza in your aviary to a regulatory authority. Your avian vet should be able to help you with this.

In most cases, antiviral compounds cannot be administered to the bird unless it is approved by these regulatory authorities. Even the vaccination that is used on your birds needs to be approved by the USDA or by the state veterinarian.

Diseases caused by parasites

There are both endo and ectoparasites that can affect Finches. These parasites are mostly found in unhygienic conditions. While they are not always fatal, there are chances that the symptoms only become obvious when the bird is already very unwell. That is the only reason why parasitic infections are a threat to the bird's life. In most cases, a bird seems completely normal and the symptoms become severe overnight.

Here are a few parasitic infections that Gouldian Finches are most susceptible to:

Coccidiosis

This condition is caused by a certain parasite that is usually found in the intestinal tract of birds. The disease is transmissible and is passed on through the feces or through interaction. The condition is highly contagious and you will notice several birds being infected immediately after you notice the first case in your aviary.

Symptoms of coccidiosis

- The vent area is wet
- The bird has consistent diarrhea
- The feathers are fluffed up
- The bird has very little energy when you approach him
- The bird tends to sleep a lot

Treatment

- A course of sulfonamide or sulphadim is required.
- The cage needs to be cleaned regularly to prevent any sort of infestation in your aviary.

- The drinking containers should be made only from glass or plastic while providing any antibiotics.

- You may continue a course of broad spectrum antibiotics.

Parasitic worms
If your bird is being fed any live foods, worms are easily picked up. It is therefore necessary for you to make sure that the live food that you give your bird is fresh.

Another source of parasitic worms is the droppings of birds in the aviary. If the parent bird is a carrier of parasites, they may transfer it to the young while feeding.

When you have an outdoor cage, you need to make sure that there are no droppings of wild birds in your aviary. This is the primary source of several parasites and infectious diseases.

Symptoms of parasitical worms

- Weakness
- Worms are spotted in the feces of birds
- Worms are seen in the water dishes

The disease is fatal only when the condition is not treated properly. The most common worms that affect finches are threadworms, caecal worms, tapeworms, gapeworms, tapeworms and roundworms.

Treatment

- Have a routine worm management program for your bird

- A broad spectrum wormer like levamisole can be administered to the bird

- Have your birds tested regularly

Scaly face
This is a condition that is also known as Knemidocoptes Jamaiscensis. When mites borrow into the feathers of the bird and lay eggs there, this condition is caused.

The condition gets worse when the eggs that have been laid in the feathers actually hatch. The most common way of transmission for this condition is when the parent birds feed the young. It has been observed in adult birds as well but the source of transmission is not very well known.

Symptoms of scaly face

- A scaly film is seen on the skin
- The scales may be formed on the eyes if left untreated
- Scales are seen on the legs of the bird

If you ignore this condition it will become fatal as the scales will slowly spread all over the body. The parasites are demanding and will lead to the death of the host.

Treatment

- Paraffin is administered to birds that have been affected by this condition.

Air sac mites
This is one of the most common conditions that you will see in Gouldian Finches. The mite that causes this condition is scientifically called

Sternostoma tracheacolum.

The condition affects the respiratory system of your bird, leading to
a lot of
labored breathing. The disease is transmitted during courtship and
also
when the parents feed their young.

Symptoms of air sac mites

- Coughing
- Loss of voice
- Abnormal chirping
- Labored breathing
- Fatigue

Treatment

- An insecticide is used to eradicate the mites fully.
- A spray containing ivermectin can be used in the cage.
- All birds, including the ones that are not affected should be treated for air sac mites.

These parasites have a life cycle of 6 days before which you need to make sure that your bird is treated. If the eggs hatch before treatment, the process becomes a lot more tedious and the condition progresses rapidly.

Accidents and injuries
Birds are always prone to accidents and injuries, especially when they are in an aviary. If you let your birds outside the cage, there are several things that can lead to accidents such as sharp edges of furniture, closed windows or even doors.

If your bird does suffer from an injury when he is moving around the house of if he has a fight with another bird, providing timely first aid is the key to helping your bird recover faster.

Broken wings

Broken wings are a very common injury with birds because of the fragile nature of their bones. With Finches, flight is the only mode of exercise and defense. When the wings of these birds are broken and not set properly, they tend to compromise the flight of the bird forever.

It is best that you take professional assistance if you have no experience with birds. However, providing first aid can relieve a lot of pain. If the wound is accompanied by open cuts or bruises, it is best that you call your vet immediately.

Helping a bird with broken wings

If your bird is stumbling on the floor of the cage and is holding one wing lower than the other, it could be signs of a broken wing. Here are a few things you can do if you suspect that your bird has a broken wing.

- Pick up your bird and put him in a carrier. The bird must be shifted to an area that is quiet and secluded.

- Once the bird has calmed down, check his body for any other injuries. In case of any cuts, you can clean it with an antibacterial solution.

- In case of profuse bleeding, dabbing some cornstarch on the wound can really help the bird.

- Cut a 12 inch strip of bandaging tape. This is the best option as it will not stick to the feather of the bird.
- Pick the bird up and gently hold the wing that is broken against the body of the bird.
- The bandage should be tight enough to hold the wing in place and can be secured under the wing that is intact.

- Let the bird walk around after the wing has been taped. If he is unable to walk or if he is unable to breathe, you may have to adjust the bandage.

- The bandage should be left on for about 4 weeks. You can consult your vet in order to provide the bird with supplements to aid the healing process.

- If the bird is unable to fly even after 4 week, he will have to be rehabilitated at a local facility.

Cuts and bruises

There are several causes for bruises and cuts in birds. Usually when a blood feather breaks, it bleeds quite profusely. This is the easiest form of bruise to heal.

Helping a bird with a broken blood feather

- The first thing you need to do is control the bleeding. Styptic powder or flour can help control bleeding.

- If that does not help, hold the wound down with gauze and apply a little pressure. This will keep the bleeding down till you take the bird to a good vet.

- The bleeding shaft is usually pulled out to prevent blood loss. You may do this at home if you have experience with birds. If not, it is best that you take your finch to the vet.

The next most common cause for injury is attacks by cats or dogs. This causes a lot of stress to the bird and you need to be extra cautious when dealing with this sort of injury.

Helping a bird who has been attacked

- Take him to a quiet room and keep him warm. This will help him recover from the shock of being attacked.

- In case the wound is bleeding, you can control it by applying pressure with a piece of gauze. But, be sure that you are not hampering breathing in any way.

- The bird must be taken to the vet immediately in order to avoid any chances of infection. Cat saliva is very toxic for birds.

- You need to check for any broken bones. In case of broken or wings, you can wrap them at home and then take the bird to the vet. In case of broken skull or legs, you must never try to clean it up at home.

Burns

A bird can suffer from burns accidentally if they land on a hot stove or if they touch a hot table lamp while flying around the house. It is very important that owners make it a priority to make their home safe for the bird to live in.

However, in case your bird does suffer from burns despite all the precautions, your bird will require first aid.

Helping a bird with scalds

Scalds are caused by hot liquids, chemicals and fire. In case this accident occurs in your home:

- First wash the burn with cold water and flush it for about 115 minutes.

- If it is a third degree burn, you have to rush your bird to the vet. On the way to the vey, you need to cover the affected area with moistened gauze pads.

- Contact lens saline is one of the most effective ways to cool down a burn as long as it is preservative free.

Helping a bird with electric burns

This is very rare in Finches as they do not have beaks that are strong enough to bite through electric wires. Nevertheless, they may come in contact with exposed live wires that may lead to the burn. Here is what you can do if your bird has an unfortunate accident:

- Do not touch the bird till you get the bird out of contact with the electrical wire. This puts you also at the risk of electrocution. Turn the electrical source off before you do anything.

- Check the breathing of your birds as well as the heartbeat. It is advisable that you learn basic CPR techniques for birds from your vet.

- Call the emergency clinic immediately. When you are taking your bird to the facility, make sure that you keep him in a container that is warm and dark. You can use a plastic bag filled with warm water to give the bird the warmth it requires.

What you must NEVER do in case of burns
- Never apply ice on the burnt area
- Butter, ointment and grease should never be applied.
- If there are any wounds with debris, do not attempt to clean them.
- Blisters should not be popped.
- Never cover a burn with a towel or any material that has fibres which may stick to the wound.
- If the bird is unconscious, do not give him any oral medications or even water.

After the bird has been treated make sure that you give him all he IV fluids and electrolytes mentioned by the vet on a regular basis. Antibiotics should be provided as required to make sure that your bird heals fast.

Toxicosis
Toxicosis or heavy metal poisoning is very common in birds. This is mostly because birds are easily poisoned by certain heavy metals like lead, zinc and iron that are found in their environment.

Each of the metals affects the birds in a different way but every one of them is equally hazardous to the bird and must be treated immediately.

Today, people are more aware of the potential issues related to metal poisoning. They take a lot more precautions to make sure that their birds are not at the risk of developing any form of toxicosis.

Like humans, birds also contain a moderate amount of zinc and iron in their body. These minerals are present in their food and are actually necessary for metabolism to occur normally. However, when the levels of these minerals increase to an abnormal level, toxicosis occurs.

Lead poisoning is the least common type of heavy metal poisoning today as most of the pet owners take precautions. You also have better quality toys and enclosures that prevent toxicity in birds.

In case the level of iron increases in the body of your bird, it leads to iron storage disease. This leads to excessive iron deposits on the internal organs of the bird. This leads to problems in the liver and can potentially damage the other organs permanently.

Symptoms of toxicosis

- Tremors
- Constant thirst
- Regurgitation of consumed water
- Listlessness
- Fatigue
- Depression
- Lack of coordination in the muscles
- Seizures

Diagnosis of toxicosis

- An X-ray of the gizzard helps identify the type of metal that has affected the bird.
- Blood tests are necessary to detect heavy metal poisoning
- If you suspect any chances of heavy metal poisoning, it is necessary that you take your bird to the vet immediately.

Treatment

- There are certain organic compounds called chelates that are used to detoxify any poisoning in the bird.

- These agents can be injected directly into the muscles of the bird to make sure that the blood level returns to normal.

- After the bird recovers from the condition, you can provide oral chelating agents.

The speed of recovery depends entirely on the level of poisoning. You can take preventive measures as well:

- Make sure that you remove any material such as the fencing or the perches and cages that may contain lead or iron.

- Stainless steel is the best option to prevent toxicosis in birds.

- When your bird is playing outside the cage, you need to ensure that no heavy metal is available for the bird to consume.

- Keep stained glass, old paints, fishing weights and lead curtains away from the bird's environment.

- You must also make sure that your bird does not come in contact with any soldered parts or areas.

Reproductive diseases

There are a few complications that may occur when your birds reach the breeding age. Particularly in the hens, there are several problems related to the formation of the eggs and the laying of eggs that you need to be aware of in order to have a healthy clutch.

Egg yolk peritonitis

This condition leads to the presence of some egg yolk in the coelomic cavity. The egg yolk is one of the best mediums for bacteria to thrive in and is usually caused by a prior bacterial infection.

The response is inflammatory and you will be able to see abdominal distension in birds that deal with this condition. In most cases, diagnosis is only possible after the death of the bird.

There are several other conditions that occur with egg yolk peritonitis including oviduct prolapse, double yolks, internal laying of the egg and internal ovulation.

You need to make sure that you follow the right lighting recommendations for your bird and also provide them with the nutrition that they require in order to lay the eggs successfully.

This condition is very common in birds that are overweight or have erratic periods of ovulation.

Symptoms of egg yolk peritonitis

- Loss of appetite
- Respiratory distress
- Fluffing of feathers
- Loss of voice or vocalization
- Depression
- Weakness
- Swollen vent
- Swollen abdomen
- Ascites

When the bird shows the symptoms, it is usually accompanied by very obvious nesting symptoms. Diagnosis upon the death of the bird reveals that the fluids contain ascites which are not present in healthy specimens of finches.

This condition usually ends in the death of the bird and is sudden or very quick in progression.

Chronic egg laying
Birds require certain nesting conditions in order to breed and lay eggs. The factors that contribute the most towards stimulating a bird to lay eggs are:
- Rainfall
- Behavior of the mate
- Availability of food
- Length of the day
- Competition for nesting areas

If the ideal conditions are available, female Finches do not even have to mate with a partner in order to lay the eggs. This leads to a condition known as chronic egg laying which can lead to other complications such as calcium depletion or hypocalcemia as well as egg binding.

Preventing chronic egg laying

You can make sure that your bird does not lay eggs by making the ideal conditions unavailable. Here are a few things that you can do:

- Allow your bird to sit on the eggs and hatch them. If you take away the eggs as soon as they are laid, she may continue to lay them. It is advised to leave the eggs in the cage until the bird loses interest in them.

- Nesting material should be removed from the cage. Things like paper and small dark places like boxes or sleeping tents should be removed. If your bird is let out of the cage, discourage him from going behind the microwave, under the table etc. where it is dark and cozy. They may even turn this into a nesting area if you do not pay enough attention.

- Keep the lights in the living area of the birds dim. It is good to increase the dark hours to make the bird feel like the days have become shorter. This will turn their breeding hormones off and will make them sleep for longer.

- Food access can be limited. In the wild, birds will never breed unless they have ample food. If your bird has the habit of laying eggs too often, you can reduce the amount of time that food is available. Instead of keeping the food bowl filled all day, you can reduce the time of food availability to 12 hours. If that does not work, you can speak to your vet to give your bird an austerity diet which is very low in protein. Giving your bird this diet for about 2 weeks will discourage breeding and egg laying.

- Do not encourage any breeding behavior in your birds. Lifting the tail, rubbing the vent etc. should be avoided. Make sure your birds get good exercise and keep them engaged.

- If nothing works, you can give your bird a hormonal injection after consulting your vet.

The one thing that you need to remember when your bird displays excessive egg laying is that it causes a rapid depletion in the nutrients in the body. Consulting your vet to provide your bird with necessary supplements can help prevent secondary health conditions and infections.

Egg binding
This is a very common but potentially hazardous condition for birds. When the female bird is not able to pass the egg through the cloaca, this condition occurs. Sometimes, the egg may be painfully lodged deeper into the reproductive tract. This condition is most common in small sized birds such as finches. If the egg breaks internally, it may even lead to the death of the bird.

There are several causal factors for egg binding such as:
- Low levels of calcium in the blood
- Limited sunlight
- Unavailability of vitamin D3 in the diet
- Malnutrition
- Lack of exercise
- Small cages that do not permit movement
- Age of the bird
- Prior illness
- Solitary laying of the eggs

Symptoms of egg binding

- Depression
- Straining of the abdomen
- Fluffed feathers
- Loss of appetite
- Abnormal droppings
- Inability to excrete

A bird with egg binding must be taken to a vet immediately. If your vet is able to feel the egg through a regular physical examination, then it is removed easily. In case the egg is deeper in the reproductive tract, an X ray is necessary to determine the condition.

101

Treatment

- If you have any doubt that the bird may have egg binding, you could keep her in a warm room. A steam room or even a warm towel can help relax the vent of the bird and aid the passing of the egg.

- A shallow water bath with warm water will help the bird to a large extent.

- Provide the bird with calcium supplementation.

- You may apply a lubricant in order to aid the passing of the egg. Coconut oil can be of great assistance.

This is a condition that can be potentially life threatening. Taking preventive measures is the best way to help your Gouldian Finch. You can provide your bird with a regular dose of calcium shots. In case you want to safeguard your bird from this condition, having them spayed is an option. If that is not an option, you can also ensure that the right breeding requirements are not available to the bird.

Your vet should also be able to provide your bird with Lupron shots which will prevent the breeding hormones from being produced.

3. Finding the perfect avian vet

Birds are extremely different from other pets. The anatomy and the basic requirement of these creatures is very different. So, you need to have a certified avian vet who can help your bird.

Avian vets have a degree in veterinary medicine but have dedicated a large portion of their practice to birds. Every country has an association that vets can register under to stay updated about this science. One such association is the Association of Avian Vets or AAV. You can find all the registered avian vets in your vicinity using their official website which is www.aav.org.

If you are unable to find a good avian vet on this website, you have the option of asking a regular vet for leads. You may also contact Gouldian Finch clubs in your city for more information.

When you are choosing an avian vet, here are a few things that you need to look for:

- Staff that is trained to handle birds. They will be comfortable around your birds and will know a little bit about the species as well.

- There should be an emergency facility linked with the clinic in case your bird needs immediate attention. It is best to look for a clinic that even has a pet hospital for in house patients.

- The vet should have mostly avian patients. If he is only seeing one or two birds in a day, he is most likely not an avian vet. Some of the avian vets also deal with exotic pets like reptiles but will dedicate most of their practice to birds.

- Each examination should be for at least 30 minutes. If the interval between each patient is just about 15 minutes, your bird may not be getting a thorough examination.

- The clinic should be as close to your home as possible. Drives are extremely stressful for pets and should be minimal.

Your avian vet should also be updated with the facilities available for birds. If he is part of the AAV or attends regular seminars about avian medicine, you can be sure that your bird is in great hands.

Chapter 7: Cost of Keeping Finches

While it may seem like financial commitments may not be as taxing as it is with pets like dogs, Finches are actually quite expensive. Below is a break up of all the monthly costs that you are likely to incur with your finches.

- Cost of the bird: A Finch that is hand raised is more expensive and will cost anything between $50-$100 or £25-£75 depending upon the age and the breed of the bird. You will also see cost differences based on where you source the birds from. Hatchlings that are parent raised are less expensive.

- Cage: This is the first big expense. It is best that you make no compromises on this as it is only a one time investment. A good cage should cost you anything between $150-$400 or £80-£200. The size, the construction material and the quality will determine the cost. A cage that is poor in quality may have traces of lead. So, you must make sure that you only get the best for your bird.

- Food: Including the fresh produce, the treats and the pellets, bird food should cost about $50 or £25 every month. In case you do not store the food properly, you may incur additional expenses because of extensive food wastage.

- Toys: You cannot deprive Finches of toys. They need them to stay mentally stimulated and grow healthily. The quality of the toys and the frequency of purchase determines the cost of the toys. On an average a pet owner will at least spend $10 or £8 on the toys purchased for his Finches.

- Veterinary costs: This is the most expensive part of Finch care. Every visit will cost you at least $50 or £40. In a year, you will shell out close to $1200 or £700 every year on veterinary care for your bird.

- Insurance: You can opt for various types of covers for your bird. Even the simplest insurance plan will cost about $150 or £80 every month. This can go up to $280 or £150.

You need to shell out close to $450 or £250 every month on your bird. These are only the basic costs. You may want to get your bird groomed or indulge your bird with toys. That will put the price bar higher.

Only when you are able to make this commitment and ensure that you will not make any compromises on the health of the bird should you bring one home. Remember, if you have a pair of Finches, the time that you need to spend with them may be halved but the cost of raising them doubles.

Conclusion

When you bring home a Lady Gouldian, remember that these birds are different from other birds like Parrots. They make wonderful pets because of their goofy personality and their beautiful voice. However, as we have discussed in the book, do not attempt to handle them too much as you would simply stress the bird out.

Hopefully, with this book you have a better insight about these unique birds. The more you learn about your pets, the better care you will be able to provide. While this book is the foundation and has just about everything that you need to know, make sure that you keep looking for any new information about Finches to stay updated.

Thank you for choosing this book. The goal is to make sure that everyone who brings home a pet is responsible for its well-being. With the number of pet birds that are abandoned or simply released into the wild, the fact that you chose to read up and learn more about these birds shows that you and your birds are about to embark on a wonderful journey together.

References

As mentioned before, the more you learn about Gouldian Finches, the better care you will be able to provide. The internet consists of several blogs and online forums that will help you learn more about these birds and stay updated.

Note: at the time of printing, all the websites below were working. As the internet changes rapidly, some sites might no longer be live when you read this book. That is, of course, out of our control.

www.gouldianfinches.eu
www.trails.com
www.finchstuff.com
www.birds2u.info
www.beautyofbirds.com
www.birdsinbackyards.net
www.panique.com.au
www.thespruce.com
www.mfgouldianfinches.com
www.abc.net.au
www.ehp.qld.gov.au
www.ladygouldianfinch.com
www.windycityparrot.com
www.lady-gouldian-finch-breeding-expert-guide.com
www.blogs.thatpetplace.com
www.planetaviary.com
www.thesplendidbourkebirdblog.blogspot.com
www.martybugs.net
www.blog.cincinnatizoo.org
www.birdingblogs.com
www.legalleadersblog.com/tag/gouldian-finch/
www.gouldian-finches.com
www.australianmuseum.net.au
www.australiangeographic.com.au
www.petassure.com
www.mourningdaily.com
www.rarefinch.com

www.arkive.org/gouldian-finch/erythrura-gouldiae
www.australianfinches.com
www.australianwildlife.org
www.finchinfo.com
www.earthsfriends.com
www.birdchannel.com
www.blogs.thatpetplace.com
www.finchaviary.com
www.studentswithbirds.wordpress.com
www.trinesty.com
www.destinyink.com
www.efinch.com
www.thefinchfarm.com

www.ingramcontent.com/pod-product-compliance
Lightning Source LLC
Chambersburg PA
CBHW060119050426
42448CB00010B/1949